READING
through play

The easy way to teach your child

by
Carol Baker

with foreword by
Betty R~~t

GW00372104

SIMON & SCHUSTER

LONDON • SYDNEY • NEW YORK • TOKYO • SINGAPORE • TORONTO

For Peter, Emily and my parents

Contents

First published in Great Britain in 1980
by Macdonald & Co (Publishers) Ltd

Reprinted in 1990
by Simon & Schuster Young Books

Simon & Schuster Young Books
Simon & Schuster Ltd
Wolsey House, Wolsey Road
Hemel Hempstead, Herts HP2 4SS

Printed and bound by
Wing King Tong Ltd, Hong Kong

© Carol Baker 1980

© in the illustrations
Macdonald Educational 1980
© in the illustrations
Simon & Schuster 1990

Reprinted 1981, 1982, 1983, 1984,
1986, 1987, 1990

ISBN 0 7500 0756 7

Foreword

Many years ago, when I was a young inexperienced teacher, I considered that teaching was for teachers. It was difficult at that time to remain patient with enthusiastic, caring parents who felt the need to be involved with helping their children to read.

Times have changed—and so have I! Being both a teacher *and* a parent rapidly modified my views. Of course we all want our children to read! The role that parents play is a vital one. Without the support of the home, teachers in schools are inevitably limited in what they are able to accomplish. Moreover, I firmly believe that children who are willing and able to make a start before school should be encouraged to do so.

It should not be assumed that *all* children will want to 'learn to read' but those who show a strong interest in the actual words in books, and in the words all around them, can be encouraged in an informal yet planned way.

Throughout all the pre-school years, sharing books with children is absolutely essential. The importance of this activity, which after all brings immense pleasure to children and parents, should not be underestimated.

In addition to book reading it is possible to provide a programme of reading games. This excellent, practical book provides parents with ideas on how to harness children's interest in reading. More specifically, this book helps parents to teach. It dispels all the mystique which has surrounded the teaching of reading in the past. The ideas put forward do not involve expensive materials and very little money is required to prepare the activities suggested. *What is required is parents' time, patience* and *concern.*

Should playing these reading games develop into an unpleasant experience; if the child is not enjoying success, then parents must be sufficiently sensitive to the situation and stop immediately.

Helping your child to read must be an exciting shared adventure.

Betty Root
Centre for the Teaching of Reading,
University of Reading.

I am interested in teaching my child to read but . . .
. . . . read on, this book is for you. Many parents are interested in teaching their children to read but feel overwhelmed by the problems that appear to surround reading:

Where do I begin?
What method do I use?
Might I do more harm than good?

We have been so conditioned to depend on experts and professionals that we lose the courage to believe in our own feelings and common sense. But remember where your child is concerned *you* are the expert. You know his special interests, his moods and needs. You also have the time and opportunity to help your child in a loving one-to-one relationship.

This is not a handbook for the competitive parent anxious to produce an academic prodigy. It is for ordinary parents who want to help their children develop their full potential and who believe that reading is within the child's grasp if presented in the right way.

Introduction to Reading Through Play

This book shows how to help your child learn to read by playing structured games. It demonstrates that, given basic information and good sense, a parent can cover the groundwork of reading, if the child is ready.

Incidentally, throughout this book the word 'he' has been used when referring to a child. Attempts to avoid this conventional use of the masculine pronoun sadly proved cumbersome and distracting. It is to be hoped that, those of you who—like myself—are parents of daughters will be tolerant of this usage.

The chapter *Getting Things Clear* (page 12) explains the general principles of reading. Familiarise yourself with this before starting the games. The games can all be made at home using easily available materials.

A wide range of play activities is important for a child's development as a complete and happy individual. Such activities are also vital for developing the language, concepts and skills that are the basis for reading. For this reason a section of this book is devoted to *Pre-reading Activities* (page 20) which should be within the reach of most children. Even if a child goes no further than this he will have covered a lot of the groundwork for reading skills.

In a child's world there is no distinction between playing and learning: play is the means by which he makes discoveries and learns about the world. Learning to read through games enables a child to learn in a way that is natural and enjoyable to him.

When should a child start to read?
'When he is ready,' is the right but perhaps not very helpful answer as children develop at different rates. Traditionally they begin to learn after starting school. This is not because 5 or 6 years old is necessarily the best age for all children to learn. In fact, when you consider the wide discrepancy in the ages at which they begin to walk or talk, it would be very curious if all children reached a point of reading readiness at nearly the same time. The truth is that many children are ready to read before 5 —some of them long before—but they are generally deprived of the opportunity.

It is now increasingly recognised that where the child is ready, reading can be successfully learned in the context of a loving home relationship.

4

So when, if at all, should you teach your child to read?
Let us first deal with this uncomfortable word 'teach' with its suggestion of formal instruction. A small child should not be taught to read in a formal way. Your aim should be to provide opportunities in which your child can learn in a happy and unpressured environment. You open doors for him but he chooses whether and when he goes through them. But you can be fairly sure that, if he is ready, and you make learning attractive, your child will *want* to learn because children enjoy mastering new skills.

The following questions are intended as a rough guide to find out whether your child may be ready to learn. If you can say 'yes' to them it is worth trying the first reading games.

Can your child:
● Speak in sentences?
● Pronounce words fairly clearly?
● Enjoy stories, poems and songs?
● Remember and repeat simple rhymes and songs?
● Understand and carry out simple instructions?
● Tell a simple story?
● Do easy jigsaws and games that require recognition of shapes and pictures?
● Play constructively with bricks and assembly toys?

Are you also satisfied that his sight and hearing are normal and that he is a happy and healthy child without any unduly worrying physical or emotional problems?

If you start the games and your child enjoys them, continue at the pace that suits him, but if he cannot manage put them away and try again in a few weeks or months. Depending on how ready the child is for reading it may take several months or even years to work through the games. No two children are alike and you should let the child set the pace. It is very important not to put the child under pressure.

Is a parent the right person to teach his own child?

Unfortunately there is a tendency to regard parents as well-meaning but inadequate individuals unfit to make any very serious contribution to their child's development. And so, underestimated by society, many parents in turn underestimate themselves. They hold back for fear of 'making a mess of things' and both parent and child miss out on the interest and delight of sharing learning adventures together.

This is a great shame, for when it is handled with sensitivity, learning together can considerably strengthen the child-parent bond. Becoming involved in a child's development and thinking of ways to interest and help him can provide many insights into his world and the parent becomes a learner as well as a teacher.

Of course, teaching your own child requires a lot of tact, and success depends on happy co-operation—never allow a battle of wills to develop. Adapt the suggestions to suit your child and be prepared to abandon a game if he is not in the mood.

As a parent you have many advantages. You can provide a happy and secure learning environment. Your special knowledge of your child enables you to recognise the best time and way to approach these games. If you are already enjoying conversations, books and games together, then reading will take its place as a natural extension of these activities. You can relate the games to the child's particular interests and make reading a meaningful part of his world. By learning with you, at home, a child does not get the idea that reading is a strange process that happens in another place. It is firmly established as part of his daily home life.

But probably the greatest of your assets is time. At school your child may well be one of 20 to 30 children competing for the attention of one adult. Given that there are about four hours of classroom time in an infant's school day, each child in a class of 25 can, in theory, receive just under 10 minutes individual attention daily. Of course time cannot be handed out in tidy units and in practice he may well receive far less than this. However busy you may be, *you* have more time to give!

Why Teach Through Games?

Teaching reading through games may at first sight appear to be a somewhat indirect approach. Why not follow a more obvious method like regular 'drill' with word cards or a reading book? Why not? Because the aim is not just reading but the *enjoyment of reading*. Holding up word cards or stumbling through a book can too easily become boring and frustrating. It is vitally important that early reading experiences are positive and happy ones. Learning to read without pleasure is a sterile achievement.

When learned through games, reading takes its place naturally in a child's daily activities and does not become a thing apart. A child should not be conscious that he is learning something 'special'. He is *absorbing reading as a by-product of play*.

When playing together parent and child are relating in a relaxed and co-operative way. There is no teacher-pupil or superior-inferior relationship. Many children who would resent any attempt at formal teaching from a parent will respond happily in this situation and will simply enjoy playing the games.

Games also protect a child from any feeling of failure. If he finds a game difficult then either you should help him with it, adapt it to suit him, or put it away tactfully. *The child should not feel that he is failing or displeasing you.*

Learning to read requires a lot of regular repetition in order to 'fix' and practise new words. *Games take the boredom out of repetition.*

Games also encourage reading for understanding. For example, in the Hide and Seek game (page 53) if a child reads the words correctly he is rewarded by the satisfaction and pleasure of finding the object. Looking at word cards or a book does not provide the same motivation to read and be accurate.

The games are arranged so that they *introduce and test only one or two skills at a time.* There is no danger of the child being overwhelmed by more than he can manage.

By using games you are less likely to find yourself at odds with methods that may be used at school.

With more than one pre-school child you will have to seize the moments of peace whenever you can. Perhaps several children can play the games together, each at his own level.

9

Reading at School

Even though their children are ready to read and they would like to help them, parents may hesitate to teach reading because they are uncertain about how this will fit in with school. Let us look at some of the questions that may arise.

Will the child be confused by a different approach to reading?

Because you have not 'taught' in a formal sense there should be no problem about clashing. Whatever your child has learned at home will be confirmed and reinforced by what he learns at school since the basic factors of reading remain the same regardless of the method of teaching.

Does it matter what stage the child has reached with his reading?

No. Whether he simply enjoys looking at books with you, is part way through the reading games, or can read easy books to himself, the important thing is that he is happy and confident at whatever stage he has reached.

If he can read already will my child have to waste time waiting for the rest of the class to catch up?

He should not have to. Teachers expect a variation in development and capabilities amongst their pupils and they allow for this by providing individual work appropriate to the needs of each child. It may be helpful if you show your child's teacher the books that he reads at home.

The children in this reception class are practising pre-reading skills which could also be enjoyed at home.

Should I continue to teach my child when he gets to school?

This largely depends on whether the child wants to carry on playing the games. If he does there is no reason to stop him. But you may find that the effort of coping with the new social, emotional and mental demands made by school tire him and make him less enthusiastic, in which case let it rest. If you are concerned, discuss the matter with your child's teacher who may suggest ways that you can supplement work done in class.

However you resolve this question, continue to take an interest in your child's development in which you still have a vitally important part to play. Carry on reading to him, enjoying his company and providing a loving and stimulating environment.

Reading apart, do help your child to be as independent as possible about looking after himself before he gets to school. Struggling with nearly 30 lots of shoes, socks, zips and buttons before and after every P. E. lesson is hard work for teachers.

Are there any disadvantages in a parent teaching his own child?

Yes, there can be. There are two main areas in which difficulties may occur.

There is a chance that a parent may make a basic technical error; for example, using capital letters instead of small letters or pronouncing the names of letters instead of their sounds. Such points are outlined in this book and avoiding them is largely a matter of common sense.

The emotional relationship between parent and child can also present difficulties. A strained or stressful relationship is not conducive to happy learning. If you and your child do not get on well together or are going through a difficult patch it is probably better to forget about reading until the relationship is right.

Even loving and caring parents can do their child the disservice of loving and caring too much. By being over-concerned about his progress they create a stressful situation in which the child may feel anxious about failing or disappointing them.

But a child who is allowed to learn at his own rate surrounded by *hugs, happiness* and *humour* can ask for no better start.

When should I give my child his first book?

From a very early age your child will enjoy looking at and being read to from books that please the eye and nourish the imagination. He should have books of his own that he can keep returning to as well as a changing selection from the library.

By playing the games in this book the child will become familiar with many words and will begin to enjoy looking for them in his own books.

The sense of achievement that he will get from being able to 'read' a book will do wonders for his confidence.

Details on choosing the first reading book are on page 87.

Getting Things Clear in Your Own Mind

Before attempting the reading games there are a few points that you should be clear about in your own mind. Once you are familiar with the basic principles and approach to the teaching of reading you will find it much easier to adapt the games to suit your particular child and circumstances.

Methods of Teaching Reading

There are many different methods but two are most frequently used. They are the Look and Say method, sometimes known as the Whole Word or Sight method, and the Phonic or Sound method. These two methods are sometimes used on their own but are more often combined. There is also the Whole Sentence method.

Look and Say Method

This is the method by which a child learns to recognise a word by sight after looking at it a number of times. He memorises the whole word without knowing the letters that make up the word. Look and Say enables a child to build up a bank of sight words far more quickly and at an earlier age than if he had first to learn the sounds of each letter and then, how to blend these sounds into a complete word.

He can also learn the words that he really wants to use which helps develop motivation and confidence in reading.

Because repetition is necessary to 'fix' the words, Look and Say is sometimes criticised as boring. This can be true if word cards (sometimes called flash cards) are just held up for the child to recognise as a kind of drill. But using the words in games makes the repetition fun and provides a more realistic context for learning.

One disadvantage of Look and Say is that there are probable limits to the number of words that can be memorised in this way. But its most serious drawback is that it makes a child dependent on someone else to tell him each new word. He has no tools with which to decipher a word for himself. And this is where the Phonic method comes in.

Whole Sentence Method

This is like the Look and Say method except that the child memorises an entire sentence usually accompanied by a picture. The Whole Sentence method helps to train the child to read from left to right and, most importantly, *to read for meaning*, because the words are seen and heard in a familiar context.

grocer   guard

fishmonger   footballer

greengrocer

gardener   hairdresser   jockey

A page from a book of words and pictures for a child to learn by the Look and Say method.
(From *Words and Pictures People* by *Margaret Clarke*)

Mrs. Blue-hat saw the mouse.

In this page from a Whole Sentence reader the child will memorise the whole sentence and recognise it on sight—aided by the picture clues.
(From *Roger and the Little Mouse* by *Sheila McCullagh*)

13

Phonic Method

A written word is made up of letters or letter groups and a spoken word is made up of the different sounds of these groups blended together. With the Phonic approach a child learns how words are made up of these smaller units. Once a child has acquired this information he is able to de-code new words for himself and finally achieve reading independence.

Ideally, Phonics are taught after the child can recognise a number of words by the Look and Say method. He reads a familiar word aloud and hears how it is made up of separate sounds. He can then apply this knowledge to other words. Thus, once he has understood the construction of **cat** he can transfer this learning to **can** and **cap**, or **hat** and **bat**.

It must be stressed that young children may not be sufficiently mature to hear the difference between similar sounds, so be prepared to delay the Phonic games until your child can cope with them easily.

Occasionally, reading is taught from the beginning by the Phonic method.

Thus a child learns the sound and shape of each letter and how to blend letters into a unified sound before he is let loose on a whole word. This can be extremely dreary and limits his early reading to words which follow a regular spelling pattern, such as dog, log, pig, jig. This prevents a child from using and reading the words that really interest him. A totally Phonic approach may also fail to train the eye to see a word as a whole unit because the child is concentrating so much on individual letters. This can make for slow and not very fluent reading and also prevents the child from using contextual clues.

For these reasons, Phonics are most effectively taught after a child has used the Look and Say method to acquire a good sight vocabulary, confidence, enthusiasm and a general understanding of the basics of reading.

Look and Say is rather like a lift while Phonics are like stairs. A lift is an easier way to get from floor to floor but when it breaks down it is vital to know where the stairs are and how to use them.

King Dan, the Dane,
came down the lane,
with baker Jake
and Jan and Jane.

In this Phonic reader the language is controlled so that it is easy for a child to transfer his knowledge of certain words to others that are new to him but which look and sound similar.
(From *King Dan, the Dane* by *Terry Reid*)

Putting it Together

In general, a child begins to learn about reading when he sees lines of print in a simple story book or the captions you have written under his own pictures. When you run your finger under the writing and read it to him he becomes aware that writing communicates interesting ideas. Later, he recognises individual words and then he learns about letters and sounds. Thus at each stage the child is absorbing information that is always related to something he already knows. This provides a secure framework for new knowledge and encourages confidence.

The reason for learning to read through these methods, instead of starting by learning letters, can be likened to a child learning to use a construction toy. If you show your child a ready constructed toy and then help him to dismantle it in a logical way, he is then in a better position to reconstruct the pieces than if you were to place a pile of pieces in front of him and expect him to build the toy without ever having seen the finished construction.

Games in this Book

The early reading games in this book are based on the Look and Say approach coupled with the Whole Sentence method, the later ones use Phonics. This particular combination of methods is frequently used in infant schools. It is also a combination which we frequently use as reading adults. An accumulation of reading experience enables us to instantly recognise familiar words by the Look and Say or Whole Word method. Only when we come across unfamiliar or difficult words and names do we have to resort to breaking a word down into its letter sounds.

The two methods are complementary and there is room for overlap between them. Once your child is making good progress with the Look and Say games introduce him to some of the Sound games (page 69 and 70). This will develop his ability to distinguish different sounds and prepare him for the Phonic games. Likewise, when introducing him to Phonics always use the familiar Look and Say words as examples whenever possible.

Mother Duck said, "Come here.
Come here, little duck.
Come and swim with me.
You can't hop!

You are not a rabbit.
You are a duck.
Ducks swim.
Come and swim like a duck."

A child can combine the Phonic approach with Look and Say and the Whole Sentence method in this new reader.
(From *I can read* by *Theodore Clymer*)

(All these readers are shown at approximately one-third of their actual size.)

aA bB cC dD eE fF
gG hH iI jJ kK lL mM
nN oO pP qQ rR sS
tT uU vV wW xX yY zZ

Lower-case Letters

Lower-case letters are small letters
or non-capital letters. With a few
exceptions, most of the words your child
sees in the reading games and his early
books should be in lower-case. When you
write anything for your children be sure
to use lower-case yourself and refer to
the chart if you need to refresh your
memory.

The shapes of many lower-case letters
bear little relation to their upper-case
(capital) letters; for example

a A d D e E g G

Thus to learn both is almost like
learning two alphabets. To prevent
confusion children are usually taught
only lower-case letters in the early
stages of reading unless general usage
demands otherwise. For example, it
would be pointless for a child to learn
its name as

ann or **david**

when it will normally be written

Ann or **David**

When talking to your child refer to
upper case as 'big' letters and lower
case as 'little' letters.

Word Shapes

One of the clues we use when we read
is the *shape* of the word. The shape of
a word is made up of two main features:
its length and the arrangement of up
and down 'tails' (ascenders and
descenders) on the letters.

Do not hesitate to introduce some
longer words into the Look and Say
games. You will probably find that your
child can handle a sprinkling of longer
words like aeroplane, television or
crocodile with comparative ease.

Some letters have ascending tails

b d f h k l t

and some have descending tails

g j p q y

and others have none.

a c e i m n o r s u v w x z

The position of these tails, or their
absence in a word, contributes to its
total shape.

In the caption to the picture opposite
the difficult words **giraffe** and **gorilla**
both have the same length and shape.
The reader will have to use other clues to
read the words. In this case, the picture
does not give much help.

The Sounds of Letters

Say **a b c d e** aloud.
Did you say **ay bee see dee ee?**
If so you were saying the *names* of the
letters. Or did you say **a buh cuh
duh e?** In this case you were saying
the *sounds* of letters.

When you are playing the reading
games use only the *sounds* of letters—
these are the building blocks of a word.

Consider, for example, the word **dog.**
If you spell it out using the *names* of
the letters you say **dee oh jee.** This
does not give much help in sounding the
word. If, on the other hand, you say
duh o guh you are on the way to
reading the word.

You will notice that it is impossible
to pronounce the sounds of some letters
without a trailing **uh** sound. If you say
the sounds for **b d g j w** you will find
that you cannot get rid of the **uh** sound,
but do *try* to emphasise the main letter
sound.

To check that you are saying the
sounds of letters correctly look at the
following list. Say the words slowly

and pause after each first letter. The
sound that you make before the pause is
the *sound* of that initial letter.

a	a-nt	a-pple
b	b-ed	b-ag
c	c-ot	c-abbage
d	d-ot	d-uck
e	e-gg	e-ditor
f	f-ork	f-ish
g	g-ap	g-ame
h	h-ot	h-ill
i	i-ll	i-mp
j	j-ug	j-est
k	k-ing	k-ettle
l	l-id	l-emon
m	m-an	m-itten
n	n-ut	n-est
o	o-n	o-live
p	p-an	p-ipe
q	qu-it	qu-een
r	r-at	r-ing
s	s-it	s-un
t	t-ap	t-en
u	u-p	u-tter
v	v-an	v-est
w	w-et	w-indow

x does not make its true sound at the
beginnings of words. Look at these ends

x	bo-x	mi-x
y	y-es	y-ak
z	z-oo	z-ebra

Practise saying the letter sounds to
yourself, for the more accurate you are,
the better you can help your child with
the Phonic games.

You will notice that the vowels—
a e i o u—are given their short
sounds as in **at end in on up.**
Much later in the phonic work the
child will learn their long sounds
or names:

a	as in	pane	ape
e	as in	feed	even
i	as in	pine	ice
o	as in	bone	open
u	as in	tube	use

The giraffe looked at the gorilla
These animal names look similar but
sound quite different.

Reading Clues

There are other clues that a child may use to help him memorise a Look and Say word. If you are aware of these clues you will be better equipped to understand and help with any difficulties.

Context
A child can often guess at a word if he knows the words around it. For example, if he can read:
mummy got on the bus at the bus . . .
he can make a fairly inspired guess that the unknown word may be **stop**.

Picture clues
Likewise a picture accompanying a word also provides a useful clue. Where possible, help your child to use context and picture clues to work things out for himself. *Encourage intelligent guesswork.* Don't interrupt or correct immediately if he guesses wrongly. Often, a child understands the meaning of a sentence without knowing every single word. He may even correct the mistake himself next time he reads the line.

Initial and final letters
Even before he knows the individual letters a child may memorise the shape of the first or last letter of a word.

Letter patterns
Some words have a distinctive pattern of letters within the word, for example:

    cook mummy bee lolly

Word shapes
Words that have the same shape are harder to distinguish from each other. A child might have some difficulty learning to distinguish certain words for this reason.

When you are choosing the early Look and Say words try and have a variety of lengths and 'tail' patterns. This may give the child more clues for identification. The following words have different shapes which makes them easier to distinguish.

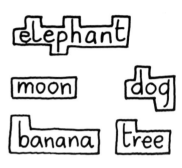

Irrelevant clues
Your child may notice that a certain word card you are using in a game has a dog-eared corner, a coffee stain or some other blemish. By associating the blemish with the word he will be able to 'read' the word without even looking at it. So keep the cards in good condition and replace any that become marked or tatty.

Key Words

These are the words which are used most frequently on the printed page. From the chart you will see that 12 words alone account for a quarter of all reading material and that these together with a further 20 words make up about a third of all reading.

    However, they are mostly small connecting words and it would be deadly boring to try and teach them in isolation. They are best learned in some context such as Labelling Pictures (page 40) the Hide and Seek game (page 53) or the Phonic games (page 68).

12

a and he
I in is
it of that
the to was

all as at be but are for
had have him his not on one
said so they we with you ₂₀

about an back been before big by
call came can come could did do down
first from get go has her here if into just
like little look made make me more much
must my no new now off only or our other out
over right see she some their them then
there this two when up want well went were
what where which who will your old. ₆₈

After Again Always Am Ask Another Any Away Bad Because Best Bird Black Blue Boy Bring Day Dog Don't Eat Every Fast Father Fell Find
Five Fly Four Found Gave Girl Give Going Good Got Green Hand Head Help Home House How Jump Keep Know Last Left Let Live Long
Man Many May Men Mother Mr. Never Next Once Open Own Play Put Ran Read Red Room Round Run Sat Saw Say School Should Sing Sit
Soon Stop Take Tell Than These Thing Think Three Time Too Tree Under Us Very Walk White Why Wish Work Woman Would Yes Year Bus
Apple Baby Bag Ball Bed Book Box Car Cat Children Cow Cup Dinner Doll Door Egg End Farm Fish Fun Hat Hill Horse Jam Letter Milk
Money Morning Mrs. Name Night Nothing Picture Pig Place Rabbit Road Sea Shop Sister Street Sun Table Tea Today Top Toy Train Water ₁₅₀

This area represents 19,750
further words. Space does not
permit the printing of these words.

The vocabulary of an average adult consists of about 20,000 different words. The chart indicates how frequently we use the words. A quarter of what we read and write is made up of the first twelve Key Words. Half of it is made up of only 100 words, as shown in the first three large boxes. Then come 150 further words which are used rather less and finally,

19,750 other words which an average adult would know but would not use as much as the others.

This 'basic word list for developing early reading and writing skills' was devised by J. McNally, Senior Educational Psychologist, Manchester and W. Murray, Headmaster, Thirlestaine Court School, Cheltenham.

Pre-reading Activities

The activities in this section should be enjoyed by all children—whether or not you intend to teach them to read. They are a necessary part of a child's development enabling him to explore and understand the world through all his senses and giving him the tools and confidence to express his own ideas and feelings. Through these activities a child absorbs and practises the skills of spoken language, visual recognition and aural discrimination, which all have a direct bearing on his ability to read. A child should continue to enjoy most of these activities long after he has started to read.

The Spoken Word

Parents are generally aware of the importance of talking to their babies from birth. Although the baby cannot understand the meaning of words he responds to the tone of the human voice and from his earliest days experiences words as part of the loving and caring that he receives from his parents.

When an infant starts using words himself he soon learns how useful they can be to him. They can help him to get things done—whether it results in getting food or his mother's attention—and provided that an attentive adult is at hand to respond to the child's words and talk to him, then his ability and confidence in handling language will grow rapidly.

Children who reach school age with a small vocabulary and who are insecure about talking are often those who have not been given this early encouragement.

A child must enjoy conversations, poems and stories before he can be expected to enjoy reading. Writing and reading are only talking and listening transferred to paper.

Encourage your child to notice the *sounds* of words. Draw his attention to words with interesting sounds like **pop buzz hiss** when they crop up in stories or conversation. Say them together— exaggerate them and relish them. Remember too, that even small children can get a lot of fun from quite long words, so do not provide a diet of exclusively simple words. Words such as automatically, transparent, aggravating may be dropped into everyday chat. Discuss new words together and let your child get his tongue round them—make it fun! Remember that you are not producing a walking dictionary but increasing your child's pleasure in words.

Rhymes and Poems

These will enable a child to build up a rich store of words and phrases and acquaint him with the *rhythms* of language. Constant repetition helps a child to feel confident about using language. Play about with rhymes. Miss words out and let your child say them. Mis-quote familiar rhymes for him to put you right:

'Jack and Jill went up to bed'.
'No! No! Jack and Jill went up the hill.'

If you find it hard to dredge children's songs and rhymes out of your memory you will get a lot of help from *Play School* and other programmes as well as books.

Help your child to recognise words that rhyme. Say a nursery rhyme or poem leaving off the rhyming words for the child to add. Can he hear that **Jill** sounds like **hill**? Think of other words together—**mill, fill, spill, Bill, will**. Once he can do this play these games:

RHYME TIME

Choose a simple word and each take it in turn to think of another that rhymes with it. You will probably have to give a young child a lot of help at first but do persevere, he is learning all the time. The game might go like this:
Child: 'Car'
You: 'Far'
Child: 'I can't think of another one.'
You: 'What do we keep our jam and marmalade in? It's made of glass and sounds like car, far.'
Child: 'Oh! Jar.'
You: 'That's right. Tar.'
Child: 'What's that?'
You: 'It's the black sticky stuff that workmen put on the roads.'

ODD BOD

List some rhyming words with a stranger amongst them, for example:
hat fat cat banana mat
fan man mix can pan
Say them slowly and see if he can spot the 'odd bod.'

Try making up silly rhymes about your child or one of the toys or pets:

John went to see
What was for tea
But O dear me
There was only a pea.

You can get away with a lot of silliness if the poem has a personal appeal!

Listening

Encourage your child to use his ears. Get him to close his eyes while you do several actions—open a door, draw the curtains, move an ornament. Can he tell you what you have done and if possible, in what order? This can be as easy or difficult as the child can manage. Let him have a go while you close your eyes.

Stop occasionally wherever you are and just listen together to the sounds that you can hear in the house, the street, the supermarket and so on.

Television and Radio

Television and radio programmes for the under fives present new information and vocabulary in a stimulating way. But to make the most of the experience you really have to stay with a very young child. You will need to translate the film or story into his own words, answer his questions and take note of new words and ideas in order to reinforce them later on.

By your presence during the programmes the child also learns how to concentrate. If you watch or listen in a relaxed and attentive way you are providing a model for the child to imitate. It is well worth encouraging wholehearted concentration rather than allowing a programme to wash over a child whilst he half plays with something else. The ability to focus the mind upon one thing will help in every aspect of learning. Remember though that the younger the child the shorter will be his span of concentration.

Instructions

We start giving instructions to a child at a very early age, 'Don't touch' or 'Open wide' as we thrust a spoonful of food at his mouth.

At a later stage you can give instructions that require a lot more of the child.

'Fetch me your boots from the kitchen.' This instruction has three distinct stages.
1. He must go to the kitchen.
2. Once there he must remember what he's gone for and find them.
3. He must bring the boots back to you.
   Don't forget to say thank you.

Looking

It may seem odd to suggest that you should teach your child to *look* at things. But if you observe people in the streets, in supermarkets or even at exhibitions you will notice how many stare around blankly.

So encourage your child to observe his environment. Discuss with him the colours and shapes of street lamps, doors, man-hole covers, supermarket displays and packaging. Help him to look carefully at natural things; flowers, leaves, insects, cross-sections of cabbages or oranges.

Ask him to notice the differences between similar things—in what ways is this leaf different from that leaf, how is new teddy different from old teddy? Such questions involve discrimination of shapes, colours and comparisons—lighter/darker, taller/shorter, fatter/thinner. Spotting small differences in similar objects encourages careful observation which will help with word and letter recognition later. Games of Snap, Picture Lotto or Picture Dominoes also help visual alertness.

SPOT THE DIFFERENCE

This game can be quickly constructed using some identical pictures from magazines or repeat motifs from wrapping or wallpaper. Alter one picture and see if the child can spot the different one.

Alternatively, draw a line of identical shapes or objects with one 'stranger' in their midst.

In preparation for later word games, you could draw a line of letters with one different from the others.

SHOW ME

This can be played anywhere and encourages the child to look at his environment.

You ask the child 'Show me a red book . . . Show me a blue car . . . Show me a white flower . . . .' The child points to the objects and then he has a turn asking you to spot things.

Talking About Pictures

Picture books will be the earliest books that your child will enjoy with you. A small child often needs help in understanding or 'reading' pictures. Guide him by asking questions about the picture or pointing things out.

Use pictures as a starting point for telling a simple story—this may only be two or three sentences for a young child. Let the child re-tell the story: it will help him to handle language and a sequence of ideas.

Encourage careful observation of detail and help the child to interpret what he sees.

'*Why* is that lady looking cross? . . . How would you feel if a dog had just stolen your dinner?' or 'What do you notice about those trees? . . . That's right, they don't have any leaves . . . What time of year is it then? . . . What do we do in the winter?'

Even the simplest pictures can be a starting point for conversation. A picture of an orange can lead to questions about colour, shape, what parts of the orange do we not eat, why does an orange have skin and pips, and so on. Together you might draw up a picture list of all the other fruits you can think of. You could even turn this into an exercise in sorting and grouping by drawing two large circles and drawing all the fruit that we peel in one and all the fruit that is not peeled in the other, or you might group fruit with stones and fruit with pips. Thus, in a simple way, the child begins to learn how to handle information by grouping, sorting and relating it to other things he knows.

This kind of approach can be used for many things. An illustration of a pair of shoes might lead to talking about different kinds of footwear—boots, slippers, clogs, sandals, flippers. Or a picture of a pair of scissors leads to a discussion of things we use for cutting— saws, lawnmowers, knives, choppers.

Obviously it would be very tedious and deadening to examine pictures in this kind of way all the time. Use this approach with discretion and only when the child is in a responsive mood.

Memory

Help your child to train his memory. Can he remember what he ate for breakfast, what the story was about on *Play School*, what Auntie Jean was wearing when she came for tea?

MEMORY GAME

Place several objects before him (only 3 or 4 if he is very young). Then when he closes his eyes you remove one of the objects. Can he tell you which one has gone? If he has difficulty with this game place the objects in a line in front of him and point to each one (from his left to right) saying its name before he closes his eyes. Let him do the same whilst you close your eyes.

Matching and Grouping

Sorting things into matching sets encourages a child to identify and categorise similar objects. It is an activity that can be made as easy or difficult as the ability of the child allows. It will be a help to him in his early maths as well as his reading.

Even a very young child can help you to sort shoes into matching pairs; sort out teaspoons from tablespoons; different coloured buttons; a mixture of butter beans, haricot beans and red beans (dried of course!)

Always check the results of these sorting activities and give praise and encouragement. If your child groups things that you would not have put together always ask him his reasons. He may be making quite valid connections between things. For example, he may place some of the teaspoons with the tablespoons because he has noticed that they have a similar pattern on the handles.

Jigsaws

Jigsaws are excellent for encouraging careful observation. Choose ones that are mounted on stiff card or wood with firmly locking pieces. A child may quickly become frustrated if pieces unlock themselves while he is working on them.

You can also make a jigsaw using a picture from a magazine, or one of the child's own drawings by mounting it on card and cutting it in to shapes. However, because of the locking problem the child may not find these very satisfying.

When the child has several jigsaws you can colour-code the back of each piece with coloured felt pens. When they get mixed up they can be sorted out by matching the colours.

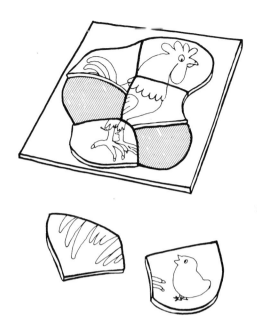

Descriptions

By encouraging a child to look at things closely you can help him to increase his vocabulary and describe his observations vividly. For example, take an illustration of a lion. Your child may tell you that it's a lion, and turn straight on to the next picture. Or he might be particularly fascinated by this picture and you can start building up a word picture together. 'Does this lion look shaggy or smooth? Is he fierce or friendly? What colour is he? So he is not just a lion any more but, 'A big golden lion with a shaggy mane.' Perhaps you can think of a name for him and make up some adventures.

You might also take it in turns to describe a picture. For example: 'The giant is fat . . . with bulging eyes . . . red hands . . . a hooked nose . . . and hairy all over!' You can also make this a memory game by listing all the things that have been said before.

Colours

So far we have assumed that a child knows his colours but this is something that you have to teach. Work on one colour at a time; red is an obvious first choice. Show the child several different things that are red—a play brick, his boots, some beads. Tell him that they are all the same colour—red. Can he find some other things that are red? If possible, set some around the room before beginning. Over the course of several days draw his attention to things that are red until this is firmly fixed in his mind. Then go on to another colour in the same way. He will also be familiar with colours by painting with them. If he uses only a few poster colours he will soon learn their names with your help.

Shapes

Does your child recognise and know the names of *circles, squares, triangles, spheres* and *cylinders*? You could introduce some of these terms if he has different shaped construction bricks.

Draw his attention to circles by cutting out several different sized circles from a piece of card. Let him play with them, colour them and grade them from smallest to largest (left to right). Point out everyday objects that are round—plates, pan lids, table-mats, wheels.

Once he has absorbed the idea of circles you can introduce him to squares and triangles over a period of time. From coloured card or gummed paper cut some squares, triangles and circles of various sizes and let the child sort them into three boxes or stick them onto three large sheets of paper. Use modelling clay or play dough to make spheres, cubes and cylinders.

Growing Things

Children can get a lot of pleasure from growing things but they need to have speedy results in order to sustain their interest. Dried peas or beans, soaked overnight and placed on wet flannel or peat, will soon begin to put out roots and shoots. Alternatively, if you can place the soaked peas or beans between a roll of damp blotting paper and the inside edge of a jam jar, the development of root and shoot can be seen even more clearly and daily progress can be marked on a strip of paper stuck to the jar.

Seeds of mustard or cress will also grow fairly rapidly on a bed of damp peat, cotton wool or kitchen paper—take care not to let it dry out at any time. If it is grown in an egg shell a child will enjoy watching the egg-head sprouting tufty green hair.

Carrot-tops placed in a saucer of water sprout pretty feathery leaves.

For the most instant effects, a child who has access to a few shrubs or even weeds can have a lot of fun making a miniature garden on the lid of a shoe box or a tray. A few twigs pressed into modelling clay make a tree; pebbles and shells make a rockery or paths and a foil tart case will serve as a pond.

If you get some seeds which sprout in jam jars—alfalfa or mung beans—the child can enjoy eating his home grown produce within a few days.

1. Leave 2 teaspoons of mung beans to soak overnight. **2.** Rinse and place in jar. **3.** Rinse twice daily and leave to grow in a sunny place. **4.** When shoots appear, lightly fry and eat as a vegetable.

Spatial Movements and Directions

Does your child understand words like *forwards, backwards, sideways, up, down, inside, outside*? He will enjoy learning these ideas about space in relation to the movements of his own body. Make a game of giving him simple instructions. 'Take 3 hops forward. Take 2 steps to the side. Take 4 rolls to the other side. Take one jump backwards.' If he enjoys this, place an object as the goal or treasure, a little distance from him and guide him to it by a series of instructions. When he reaches the goal it is his turn to call instructions to you.

It is not worth trying to teach left and right at this stage—it is far too difficult but you can help the child accustom his eyes to looking at things in a left to right direction in readiness for reading. On a large sheet of paper or a blackboard draw a cat. On the right-hand side draw a feeding bowl or a mouse. With a crayon or his finger the child draws a line from the left-hand drawing to the right-hand one. Try other drawings like car and garage, dog and bone, bird and nest, football and goal.

BATTLESHIPS

You will need
Large sheet of paper or card divided into 9 squares
Token or small toy for each player
Target (toy or picture—see above)
12 cards—6 with red on one side, 6 with blue. One colour—let's say red—indicates up or down. Draw a red line along the top and bottom of the board. Blue indicates sideways. Draw a blue line at the sides.

Aims—to give the child practice in interpreting and acting upon directional instructions—*up, down* and *sideways*—on paper.

Method
1. Place the tokens on one square, the target on a distant one.
2. First player turns over a card from the pack and moves one square up, down or sideways depending on the colour.
3. Next player has a turn, and so on.
The winner is the one to reach the goal first.
This is a simplified version of the old game known as battleships.

Music

As well as talking to your baby from birth, sing to him. It is a very relaxing form of communication and will help to develop his ear for pitch and rhythm.

An older child may enjoy singing round songs like Three Blind Mice or London's Burning. Try stopping a song in the middle for him to pick up and continue.

If you have any instruments in the house, play them. Make up stories about giants or elephants (playing heavy bass notes) and birds or fairies (high trilling notes). Encourage the child to act out these stories with dance or movement. Help him to discriminate between long and short notes, soft and loud, fast and slow. Make him a shaker with dried peas or rice.

Using a wooden spoon on an upturned pan or a table, tap out a simple rhythm using no more than three taps at first.

See if the child can imitate it. When he can do this make some taps loud and some soft and let him copy you. This takes a lot of concentration and control so do help him. Can he guess a tune when you tap or clap the rhythm?

A xylophone can be a very satisfying instrument for a child. But because the very little tinny ones can sound so awful it is worthwhile paying out for something with a reasonable size and tone. Seek advice from a good toy or music shop. You can also buy sets of chime bars.

When playing recorded music it is worth noting that babies are thought to respond best to the sound of the flute on account of its purity of tone.

Do not be tempted to dismiss music as an optional extra. Present research is establishing a connection between early musical training and reading skills. (See Bibliography, page 95, for details of materials that are available.)

my mummy

Creative Skills

Painting, drawing and modelling provide a means by which the child can discover and express his feeling and observations about the world. Unfortunately painting and gluing can quickly turn a home into a disaster area. So you will have to organise these activities to suit your convenience. However, try and keep some drawing materials constantly available.

Provide as wide a range of materials as you can. Here are some suggestions; finger paints, poster paints (if you buy the primary colours—red, blue and yellow —you can mix a good range of colours from them) large brushes, chalks, crayons, felt pens, coloured pencils (these may seem a bit drab after felt tips), gummed paper and round ended scissors, a supply of paper (lining paper from a wallpaper shop) and a black board (you can make one by painting blackboard paint onto the shiny side of a piece of hardboard).

A piece of white formica stuck on to blockboard has many uses: as a wipeable drawing board for felt pens or as a strong base for jigsaws and clay modelling.

Take an interest in your child's drawings or paintings but do not try to influence them. Your idea of art and his are quite different. If your child will talk about his pictures you will find they can provide fascinating insights into his world. Sometimes a child is so deeply involved in talking to himself about his painting that you realise that what is happening is as much an inner drama as a painting.

Whilst not trying to influence a child's art work, it is a good idea to provide opportunities to extend his techniques. A child will discover some methods for himself. Others you can demonstrate to him. If you just sit and work at some new idea beside him he will look over your shoulder and absorb whatever interests him. Here are a few suggestions for picture making:

Smudges
Put paint thickly on one half of the paper, fold over and see the image mirrored on the other half.

Dribbles
Thick blobs of paint make dribble patterns when the paper is held up and the paint runs. Make a paint blob and blow on it with a straw.

Wax resist
Draw with a wax crayon. Paint over the top and see the wax lines resist the paint. This is particularly magical if you scribble with a white crayon or a candle. The invisible scribble shows up as you brush thin paint over it.

Printing
Half carrots, leaves, corks, yoghourt cartons and pieces of sponge can all be used for printing paint onto paper— as well, of course, as the familiar halved-potatoes with shapes cut into them.

33

eggs

bowl

scales

wash hands

flour

spoon

Cooking

Cooking is a marvellous way to introduce
a child to practical maths and to extend
his vocabulary. It has the added bonus
of involving all the senses—sight, hearing,
touch, smell, taste—and the creative
satisfaction of an enjoyable end product.

Allow plenty of time for the cooking
sessions in order to get the most out
of them.

Counting You can invent any number of
simple maths exercises whilst cooking
such as counting bun cases and spoons of
sugar.

Adding There are 6 buns on that tray
and 4 buns on that tray. How many are
there altogether?

Subtraction If you and I have a bun
each for elevenses how many will be left?

Multiplication If we all have 2 buns
each how many is that altogether?

Division We have 9 buns so how many
can we each have? Will there be any left
over?

Help the child to work out the answer
visually by grouping the buns or tarts.
You can also introduce the idea of
halves, *thirds* and *quarters* by cutting
up the dough or pastry. In this way the
child learns to handle mathematical
ideas in a real and practical situation.

Other ideas that you can introduce
are *measurement*, *weight* and *volume*.
Involve him as much as possible in
measuring fluids and weighing
ingredients. Encourage him to notice
such things as $\frac{1}{2}$ lb (250 grammes) of
flour take up more room than $\frac{1}{2}$ lb
(250 grammes) of sugar; that the same
piece of pastry can look bigger or smaller
depending on whether it is rolled into a
ball or rolled flat on a table. This helps
him to form some understanding about
volume and weight.

By talking to the child as you work
together he will become familiar with
words like; **weighing, measuring,
stirring, mixing, rolling.** Encourage
him to use his senses and develop a
vocabulary for what he can:
See—pale, dark, frothy, crumbly
Hear—slurping, sizzling, popping,
bubbling
Feel—sticky, greasy, lumpy, smooth
Smell—sour, burnt!
Taste—sweet, bitter, crunchy, chewy.

Preparation
Preparing to cook can also be part of the
fun if the child is old enough to help you
assemble the things that you need. Draw
him a picture list, or if you are going to
cook together fairly often, make a card
for each of the things that you will use.
Store the cards and select the ones that
you will need for a session and let the
child help get the things together.

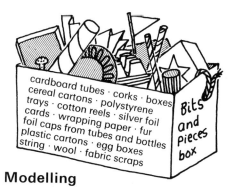

cardboard tubes · corks · boxes
cereal cartons · polystyrene
trays · cotton reels · silver foil
cards · wrapping paper · fur
foil caps from tubes and bottles
plastic cartons · egg boxes
string · wool · fabric scraps

Bits and pieces box

Modelling

Children enjoy developing their skills and imaginations using three-dimensional materials. Try to provide either modelling clay, potters' clay or play dough (see recipe below). A few simple 'tools'—a lolly stick, old teaspoon, small plastic tube and bottle lids, blunted cocktail sticks—will provide scope for scratching and pressing patterns onto the models.

Collect useful throw-outs. If they are tossed into a Bits and Pieces Box you will always have a ready supply of materials from which a child can make weird and wonderful constructions.

Try and provide a range of things for sticking and fixing—a P.V.A. glue, sticky tape, paper clips, paper fasteners. A stapler is very useful but you will have to help when using it.

Papier mâché is fun and can produce some surprisingly effective results. But it is messy and will need supervising.

Play Dough Recipe
1 tablespoon cooking oil
1 cup flour
½ cup salt
1 cup water
2 teaspoons cream of tartar
few drops of food colouring

Mix all these to a smooth paste. Cook slowly in a pan for a few minutes. Cool. Wrap closely and store in refrigerator.

To make papier mâché

1. You will need: paste, newspaper, sticky tape, scissors, cardboard tube, plastic bottle or inflated balloon.

2. Tear newspaper into strips, dip into paste and stick all over bottle or balloon.

3. When dry, stick on sections of tube for legs (and nose if using balloon). Make ears. Stick on more newspaper strips.

4. When absolutely dry, paint and varnish. Add eyes, tail etc.

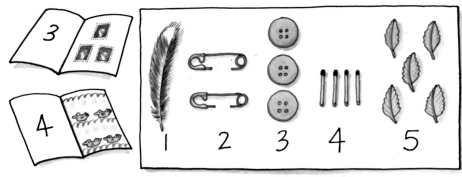

Number Books   **Number Wall Chart**

Counting Trays

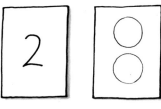

Counter Cards

Numbers are Everywhere

You will find many daily opportunities for counting aloud together: cutlery, mats and plates as you lay a table; stairs as you climb them; fingers and toes; slices of bread and biscuits. Use practical examples to do simple adding and taking away: 3 bricks on a pile add 2 more—how many is that? 4 biscuits on a plate eat one—how many are left?

Once a child is interested in counting you might introduce him to written numbers. But it is important that he understands the *idea* of numbers before seeing how they are written.

NUMBER BOOK

A well-illustrated number book or a home-made number book and wall chart will interest him at this stage. You might illustrate a home-made book with drawings, cut-outs or motifs from wrapping paper. Your child might enjoy helping you to collect and stick light-weight objects onto a wall chart.

NUMBER BOX

Give the child a box with a number clearly written on the side. If he is still uncertain about written numbers, stick an appropriate number of gummed dots on the box as a counting aid. He must find and put in the box the correct number of similar objects. If the number is 4 he might, for example, put in 4 furry things, or 4 things with wheels or 4 red things. Help him do this a few times before expecting him to try on his own. Check the contents of his box and discuss the things he has chosen.

COUNTING TRAYS

Write or paint numbers onto the inside bottoms of some containers such as baking cases or plastic tubs. Underline 6 and 9 to avoid confusion. Give the child some counters, buttons or dried beans and let him count the appropriate number into each container. Check the results and give praise. Give him some help whenever necessary.

COUNTER CARDS

You will need
   Cards approximately 4″ × 2½″ (10 × 6 cm) (one card for each number that the child knows)
   Counters, buttons or beans
   Felt pen
   Gummed dots (optional)

Aim—to practise recognising written numbers in a way that allows the child to check his own answer.

Method
1. On one side of each card write a number. On the other side stick the appropriate number of gummed dots— or draw and colour in counter-sized spots.
2. You show the child a card—number side up—and he gives you the corresponding number of counters. He can check his answers by turning the card over and placing his counters on the spots. It is better for him to check his own answers than to be corrected by you.
3. If he is right he keeps the card.
   Keep playing until he has won all the cards. Then it is your turn to play with the counters.

Water play is an important part of early mathematical understanding.

Moves Towards Reading

Marks on paper

There is a stage before learning to read in which a child must absorb certain rather abstract ideas about the nature of reading and writing. These ideas cannot be taught directly; a child must be guided towards an understanding of them. The first idea that he must grasp is the concept of the written word. It is a truly remarkable thing that one person can convey their thoughts to another by means of squiggles with no sound being uttered between them. Familiarity blunts our appreciation of just how amazing this process is and we may forget that a child has to learn this basic fact: *marks on paper have meanings*.

Help your child understand this by drawing his attention to the writing that is all around him: on toys, food packets, sign posts and so on. Let him see you write shopping lists and letters and explain what you are doing. You are not expecting him to learn to read from these examples—in general the lettering will not be suitable—but the child is becoming aware of and interested in the written word.

When you read to your child point at words and let him know that these black marks let you know what to say.

If you are using a book with large print and very few words to the page, you might single out a word that recurs frequently—perhaps the name of the main character—and show it to the child. Let him point to it and then show him the same word on another page. He might be able to pick the word out for himself next time. Only try this if he is obviously interested and does not resent the interruption to his story.

Left to right

A child also has to learn that we read words in lines from left to right and top to bottom of a page. By pointing at words as you read you can introduce

this idea. Do not try and explain left and right but let the child experience the movement of print. When you are reading to him why not tell him that your pointing finger is tired and ask if you can borrow his. Guide his finger along the line of writing. At the end of each line show him that he must take his finger off the page and 'fly' it to the beginning of the next line. Do not let him drag his finger or he will think that the reading sequence goes from left to right on one line and from right to left on the next and that could be very confusing!

A positive attitude
In addition to understanding these concepts a child is also forming an attitude to reading. If the written word plays an interesting and exciting part in his life he will have a positive outlook to reading from the start.

SHOPPING LIST

This suggestion is only practical when you are buying a few items and are not in a hurry.

Sit down with the child and a sheet of plain paper and discuss the things that you have to buy. Draw each item on the left-hand side of the paper making sure that the child understands the drawing. Then write the word on the right-hand side of the page. Tell him 'This is a picture of bread and this is the word **bread**.' Let him 'read' the list back to you. Put him in charge of the list.

When you return home fold the list down the centre so that he cannot see the pictures and see if he can 'read' the words to you. If he can, he may be simply memorising the order of the items but he is beginning to look at words and realise that they are very useful.

jam

eggs

bread

soap

sausages

cakes

apples

Making Books

You can make books quickly by stapling or stitching together some folded sheets of paper. Alternatively buy unlined exercise books or scrap books. Choose subjects that are of immediate interest to the child: my dog, things I eat, shopping, teddy's adventures, book of big things, book of round things. Use the words of the child as much as possible and let him do the drawings.

Labelling Pictures

Label your child's drawings using his own words, making sure, of course, that he does not mind you writing on his work. Use lower-case letters and say the words as you write them. Read out the title pointing to each word. Ask the child to do the same. Put the picture up where it can be seen and read often. In order to ensure a clear space for writing you might find it helpful to fold back a strip of paper and secure it with paper clips before the child begins his drawings.

You will notice that this is like the Whole Sentence method of learning to read (see page 12). At this stage, however, you are not expecting the child to learn to read these words. But he is absorbing some very important ideas about reading. He is learning that the black marks have meanings, that they are looked at from left to right and, most important, he has the excitement of seeing his very own words in writing.

Acting It Out

Act nursery rhymes and familiar stories together. The child might do the actions or use his soft toys as actors while you tell the story. Make some simple glove puppets by drawing faces onto paper bags. If these are difficult to handle stuff the bags with screwed-up

Mummy sat in the sun in the garden

easily and then try and engage his complete attention for as long as he is prepared to give it.

Although you are not yet teaching reading you are shaping his attitude to it. Because he enjoys having you read to him the child is going to be better motivated to read for himself and will have a positive attitude to books.

Remember that the most effective way of communicating the joy of books and stories is to show that you enjoy them yourself. Read to your child with expression, varying the pitch and speed of your voice to suit the story. Indulge your dramatic talents as witch, mouse or dragon!

Although it is difficult to concentrate on your own books when children are around, don't give up altogether. It is good for children to see that you enjoy books too.

paper and tie them onto a stick. You can also make simple but effective puppets by drawing faces onto wooden spoons. These are very popular with small children but don't expect to cook with them again!

The Reading Habit

It is important for a child to handle books and enjoy their pictures and stories from an early age. Try and read to your child every day or as often as he enjoys it. Choose a time when you are both relaxed—if you are wondering whether the potatoes are about to boil over and he would really prefer to be jumping on the sofa—then you are wasting your time. If your child is very active or there are other children around then you will have to be very watchful to find these good moments. If it can be made to fit into the family routine, a bedtime story is a good idea. Check that the child is comfortable and that he can see the book

Libraries

If you have a library nearby do make it a regular treat to go and browse through the children's books together. With good picture books being so expensive you could never hope to have such a wide range of books at home. The library also provides a useful opportunity for you to discover the kind of books and illustrations that your child enjoys which will guide you when you are buying books for him.

Carry on reading

For many years a child's ability to understand a story that is read to him will far outstrip his ability to read to himself with ease and understanding. So keep reading to him as long as he will let you. After all, it's a poor reward for learning to read if he can no longer have the pleasure of snuggling up to Mum or Dad and sharing a story.

Making Reading Fun

Remember that the first aim of the games is pleasure. If he enjoys them your child will want to play. If he does not, do not play. Do not attempt to force a reluctant child or the result will only be resentment and anxiety.

When to play
Only play the games when you are both happy and relaxed. If your child is coping with emotional or health problems be prepared to drop the games until he is back on an even keel.

Play when the child is neither too tired nor too active to concentrate and when you can give your undivided attention. When the situation is right try and fit in a game most days but do not feel guilty about lapses.

When to stop
Knowing when to stop the games is as important as knowing when to start them. Stop while a game is still enjoyable— do not wait for the child to become bored. Look out for any conflict in yourself between the sensitive mother who recognises that her child's interest is flagging and the over-zealous teacher who wants to progress a little further. Remember that a child cannot concentrate for long periods and that *little but often* is the best guide.

Making progress
Be prepared to find that learning may not progress smoothly and evenly. Just as physical growth occurs in bursts learning may also take place in fits and starts. The child may appear to be making no progress for several weeks or months and will then startle you with a sudden breakthrough.

As children all develop at quite different rates do not be tempted to compare one child with another. Respect your child's individual growth and development.

but a slow journey marked with significant milestones. It is almost impossible to pinpoint the exact stage at which a child becomes a reader.

Do not feel that by starting these reading games you are necessarily committing yourself to finishing them at all costs—they are not a course of antibiotics! If you do have to discontinue them you can be sure that, so long as you have both enjoyed what you have done, the results will be positive.

Keeping it fresh

Do not allow a child to get bored with the same old material. Keep updating it and make new games before the old ones begin to pall. Be fluid in your approach—change and adapt the games. Keep things fresh and lively.

Think of different ways to lead into the games. Here are three ways in which you might engage the child's interest:
● The straightforward approach—'I know a good game called . . . shall I show you?'
● Arousing his curiosity—leave the new cards or game where he will 'discover' them himself. This allows him to take the initiative and come and ask you about them.
● Imitating you—sit and play the game on your own. If he is curious and wants to join in then you let him. As with the second suggestion it is a good idea if he decides to play the game with no pressure from you.

When to correct

In general you should be wary of having to correct too often. It may be a sign that you are doing too much too soon. If this is the case, go back over old ground before moving on, or leave things for a while. Where possible, try and help your child to work out the answer for himself.

Keeping it under your hat

Unless your child *asks* to learn to read —he may want to imitate an older brother or sister—it is not advisable to tell him that you are teaching him to read. If you present reading as a goal you give the child two alternatives: he can succeed or he can fail. *He should not be put in a position where he can fail.*

By the same token you should think twice about mentioning to friends or relatives that you are teaching your child to read; friendly inquiries about progress can be irksome.

Do not ask the child to demonstrate his reading skills in front of other people unless he wants to.

The games should be undertaken for your mutual pleasure and interest. Even if your child is not reading by the time he starts school he will have acquired an interest in books and words. By taking him through these games to whatever level suits him you will have started him on the path to reading. The transition from non-reader to reader is not a sudden dash across a frontier

Getting it Together

You will find it helpful to have all the materials that you will need for the games permanently assembled in one place: a drawer, box or cupboard. It is very off-putting for a child to hang around while you rush about hunting for glue, card, scissors and ruler. It also means that if every game has to be preceded by a domestic upheaval you are less likely to fit a game into the odd ten or twenty minutes. So, however chaotic your life may be normally, it is worth making the effort to get organised once and for all. Large (used) envelopes or rubber bands are useful for keeping individual games together.

It may be easier to do the more mundane preparation of measuring and cutting cards when the child is out of the way, but he may enjoy 'helping' to make some of the things.

The materials for the games are easily available and fairly inexpensive. Keep your stocks up so that progress does not grind to a frustrating halt for want of some card or glue.

You will need

Card · Scissors · Glue
Ruler · Black felt pen
Pencil · Coloured pens,
pencils or crayons · Cut-
outs · Gummed paper dots
Paper · Notebook · Box or
large envelopes for storing
cut-outs and word cards

Cut-outs

A major part of your equipment will be cut-outs from magazines or catalogues (unless you feel sufficiently competent with a pencil to draw your own illustrations). Collect clear and colourful

illustrations of things that will be of interest to your child. The most useful cut-outs are those that will fit the word-and-picture cards, which will be about 4″ × 3″ (10 × 7½ cm). Store them in a large envelope or box and build up a good-size collection well in advance of playing the games.

The more that you can relate early reading material to the child's own life and interests, the more motivated he will be to learn. Magazines often have good illustrations of the familiar paraphernalia of everyday life: crockery and cutlery; food; toys; clothes and footwear, and many others. Capitalise on any special interest such as animals or motor cars and on passing and seasonal interests: a bus ride; making jam tarts; a summer holiday, or winter.

Where possible, use illustrations that really resemble familiar objects. For example, to illustrate the word **boots** a picture of some red wellies just like his own will have far more meaning to a child than a pair of fashion boots.

When you use the cut-outs always make sure that you both agree on the illustration. For example, what you call a flower the child might call a daisy, as with rat and mouse, or milk and bottle and so on.

A notebook
In a notebook keep a record of the words and letters that your child learns. This will be an invaluable reference point when you are planning games, writing messages or preparing for the first reading book. Also jot down any particular difficulties or problem words as they crop up so that you can give some attention to them at a later time.

Making it look good
Prepare the cards and games with care. No-one wants to handle badly cut cards with poor illustrations or oozing glue. Well chosen cut-outs, careful lettering and a little care can produce very professional results.

The final ingredients you will need are:
A sense of proportion
A sense of humour
Lots of love

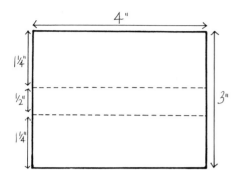

Word Cards

Word cards are the basic equipment of the Look and Say games. By playing with these your child will learn to read his first words, so they should be made with care.

To make the cards cut white card into rectangles 4″ × 3″ (10 × 7½ cm) using the diagram as a guide and write in black felt pen using lower-case letters (page 16). Store the cards in a box or strong envelope and renew them as they become dog-eared.

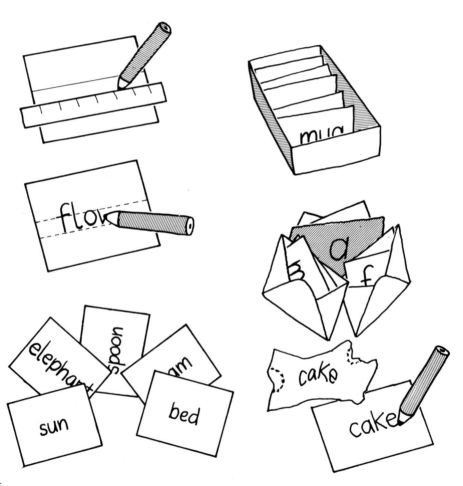

Keeping on the Right Lines

As in most things you do with your child *how* you do it is probably more important than *what* you do. The spirit in which you undertake these games will help form the child's attitude to reading. Therefore you want to be certain that you are approaching them in a positive way. The checklist below will help you to monitor your own approach. Refer back to it from time to time to check your own progress.

● Does your child's happiness come first?
● Do you keep the games light-hearted and fun?
● Do you only play when your child is willing and interested?
● Does he enjoy the games?
● Do you give encouragement and build confidence?
● Do you allow time and practice for new skills to be absorbed?
● Do you respect your child's own pace of learning and not try to force him?

● Do you stop the games before the child tires of them?
● Do you keep a sense of proportion remembering that reading is only part of a child's total development?

If you can answer *yes* to all the questions you and your child are probably having great fun with these games. If you say *no* to any, stop and re-assess the situation. Are you tackling things too early or too quickly? Or perhaps it is just that the time and the mood are wrong and, if you try again another day, they will go smoothly.

Sometimes you will find that when you have prepared a game your child may just not be interested or co-operative on that particular occasion or he may be easily distracted. Don't allow yourself to be disappointed or annoyed— that won't help either of you. A philosophical shrug is really the only answer. If you have a very active child this will happen more often than with a quieter one—but don't give up.

Reading Games–

baby | Granny

Family Words

If you have been labelling your child's pictures and pointing to sentences in picture books, your child will now be familiar with seeing words as parts of sentences. In these games you will be introducing single words as well as sentences.

How to Introduce a New Word

There is a basic sequence of events which, if followed every time you introduce a new word, will lay down the foundation for clear and logical learning.

1. When you introduce a new word tell the child 'This word is . . . . . .'
Say the word slowly and move your finger under it from left to right as you do so.

2. Repeat step 1.

3. Ask him to tell *you* the word and encourage him to point as he does. Guide his finger if necessary.

4. Praise him and ask him to do it again.

Good habits cannot begin too early and training a left-to-right eye movement is a basic requisite of accurate reading.

Prepare a supply of name cards for each member of the family. Include pets and favourite stuffed toys or dolls as well as the humans.

To start, introduce the child to his own name card as described in *How to Introduce a New Word*.

Make these first sessions very short but return to the cards as frequently as the child's interest allows. Try and find ways of maintaining interest in his name card. Before a meal he might put it at his place on the table. Or if you are saving a treat for later he can put his name against the biscuit, cake or whatever. Be as ingenious as you can about this.

Once he has grasped the idea of his own name you can show him your card **Mummy**, or **Daddy**. Introduce it in the same way as before. Then place the two cards together and ask, 'Which card says . . . (his name) and which card says **Mummy**?' Return to the card several times and if he can still distinguish them easily you can introduce a third name.

If you think extra help is needed then illustrate the cards. Draw on the backs or make the cards longer with room for a drawing alongside the word.

| Daddy | Mummy | Sooty | Coco |

This pictorial clue can be folded back or cut off when it is no longer needed.

Once a child can recognise several names let him practise using them. Here are a few ways in which they might be incorporated into the daily routine. You will doubtless think of many others.

● When you are laying the table the child could put name cards at each place.

● When you are sorting ironing into people-piles the child can label each pile.

● Before watching a programme together the child could label the seats.

● Ask the child to draw each member of the family on a different sheet of paper and place the appropriate name underneath. Why not persuade each member of the family to lie down so that you can draw life-sized outlines of them all.

These family words are the child's first experience of reading so don't be in a hurry to move on. Give him time to absorb this new information.

Use the family cards in different ways to give the child plenty of practice without becoming bored.

MUSICAL HATS

You will need
  Music that can be turned on and off (your voice will do)
  Hat
  People or stuffed toys with a name card for each.

Aim—to practise reading the name cards.

Method
1. Everyone sits in a circle with the pile of name cards face down in the middle.
2. Start the music (or singing).
3. When it stops turn over the top word and show it to the child who places the hat on the person or toy named on the card.
4. Music starts again and so on . . .

Telling a Family Story

Do you make up stories for your child? If so, you will find this game easy. If not, you may be pleasantly surprised at what you can do when you have a go.

  Shuffle the family cards and lay them in a pile face down before you. Take a deep breath and begin inventing . . . 'One afternoon when it was raining hard and the wind was shaking the apple tree' (turn up card —child reads it—**Coco**) 'Coco was hanging out of the toybox feeling as gloomy as the weather. He was remembering the good old days when he had been a bright new clown with a red pom-pom hat and he had made everyone laugh with his tricks and headstands. Now his hat was lost—probably screwed up at the bottom of the toybox—his clothes were faded and there was a slit in his leg where his stuffing was coming out. Emily's mummy had promised to sew his leg but she never seemed to get around to it. Whilst he was thinking his gloomy thoughts, Coco heard footsteps on the stairs. The door opened and in walked . . .' (turn up the next card—child reads—**Granny**) And so on, until everyone has been worked into the story. Your child will probably be a very willing turner up and reader of the name cards—anxious for his own name to appear in the story.

Using the word cards

Each time you play, go over any words that were learned in the previous session and always try to use them in sentences. A child may appear to learn a new word very quickly when it is first shown to him but the real test of learning is whether he can recall the word next time you play—and the time after that. Constantly revise and reinforce the words that he has learned already. The same words can often be used in several different games allowing plenty of practice without the child becoming bored.

Try also to widen the child's experience of new words by putting them into different contexts. For example, when he has learned **Mummy** on his word card you might ask him to do a drawing of you, or get out a photograph of yourself, then you can write **Mummy** underneath it and pin it on the wall. In addition perhaps you have a drawer, a recipe book or anything that the child knows to be specially yours on which you can stick a large label saying **Mummy**. By varying the situations in which a word is read a child gains in reading practice and confidence.

Always use the new words in written sentences as much as possible. Try to work them into picture captions, home-made books or anywhere the child will see and read them.

Do not go on to a new word until you are sure that the previous ones have been thoroughly learned.

How can you tell if a child has thoroughly learned a word? It is reasonable to assume that a word is 'fixed' in his mind if he can recognise it easily after a time lapse and if he can recognise it in a different context to the one in which he originally learned it.

51

Room Cards

Prepare some cards to be used in a room: **table—chair—window—door—cupboard.** Introduce each new word very gradually and only move on to the next new word when the previous ones are firmly learned.

Using the room words
As he learns them, ask the child to put the words in their right places in the room. Gather up the words frequently so that the child can practise setting them out again, as there is a tendency to cease looking at things that are constantly before our eyes.

Try this in different rooms to ensure that the child can relate his words **chair** and **window** to all chairs and windows.

Make some books on themes such as 'things we see from our window' or 'people who come to our door'. These can be very simple and only a few pages long, but do involve the child in helping with the story and illustrations. Alternatively, use the words in picture captions that can be pinned on the wall.

Words in Context

The following games provide various opportunities for the new words to be recognised and practised. In addition, try to introduce them into written phrases or sentences whenever you see the chance. This will help to increase the child's experience and confidence in handling these words.

MAKE-BELIEVE ROOM

Sit together in an emptyish space—on a lawn or rug—with the room cards face down in a pile. The child turns up the first room card and reads it.

If it is **door** then you both decide where your door is going to be in this imaginary room and place the card there to remind you. Go to town on the make-believe: perhaps the door creaks and needs oiling: What can you see outside your door? Perhaps the next word is **bed**. You will need to discuss where your bed must go. Try the bed out. Is it soft and springy or hard and lumpy?

Carry on until you have turned over all the room cards and created your pretend room. This is as much an exercise in conversation and drama as in reading and you will probably find that playing in your 'room' takes over from reading. This is fine, but you can keep your child on his toes by having a move around: or let him move the furniture whilst you go out. He will be delighted if he can catch you out on your return. So 'ham it up'; go to bed on the cupboard, walk out through the window. Have a laugh together.

HIDE AND SEEK

You will need
  Room cards
  Card for **the**
  Object to hide and card for it.

Aims—to practise reading room words; to introduce the word **the**; to reinforce the left-to-right eye movement.

Method
1. The child closes his eyes while you hide the chosen object in, under or near one of the places for which you have a card.

the television ···→

2. You lay out the two cards for a clue (such as **the cupboard** or **the television**).
3. Guide his eye by pointing from left to right under the words.
4. The child looks for the object in the place where the clue has directed him. If he has mis-read the clue he will soon discover his mistake and come back and read the clue again.
5. Let him hide the object and lay a clue out for you.

MIME TIME

You will need
  Room cards

Method
1. Shuffle cards and place face down.
2. First player takes a card and mimes the word for the others to guess.
   Everyone takes a turn.
   Vary your mimes. For example, for window you might pretend to clean it, open it and look out, or even break it.

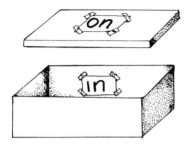

In On Under By Behind

Once your child can manage two-word clues easily you can move on to three-word clues such as **in the cupboard**, **under the chair**. But first you have to teach these rather tricky little prepositions. Do this in the following way:

Make two sets of cards for each of the words **in on under by behind**. Get a box—a shoe box with a lid or a grocery box that closes—and a blank card. First of all you want to be certain that the child understands the meaning of these words so ask him to:

'Put the card *in* the box.'
'Put the card *on* the box.'
'Put the card *under* the box.'
'Put the card *behind* the box.'

Go no further until he can clearly understand these directions. Then show the child the words **in on under** one at a time and get him to help you tape them to their appropriate place on the box. Then give him the **in on under** words from the second set and ask him to put them in their right places. The words already stuck into position act as a guide. Once these words are mastered you can add **by** and **behind** to the repertoire introducing them in the same way. These will have to be placed by the box rather than stuck on to it.

Phrase Making to Sentence Making

You can now play hide-and-seek giving phrase clues such as: **under the table**; **by the bed**. Encourage the child to point at each word as he reads it. Eventually you will be able to move on to reading a simple sentence by combining the name cards and the room cards.

To make sentence clues such as
teddy is behind the sofa
you will need to make a card for **is**. This is one of the Key Words (see page 18) which are the nuts and bolts of language but which would be meaningless and uninteresting learned out of context.

Lay out the clue, let us say
bunny is in the cupboard
Point to each word giving as much guidance as necessary for your child to read them. He then goes to find bunny. (Make sure you have remembered to put bunny in the cupboard first!)

Do not underestimate the difficulty of this activity. Once he can do this a child has made enormous progress. He will have memorised 20 or so words and will be able to read them for meaning. He will also be learning that words are useful and that playing with them can be great fun.

54

In, on, under, by, behind are all words that children understand and use from an early age.

Looking Ahead

So far your child has learned words by the Look and Say method. This means that, with practice, he has recognised words without knowing their individual letters. Later, when he plays the Phonic games, he will learn the shape of each letter, its sound, and how these sounds are blended or run together to make a whole word.

But before learning the letters, the child should be exposed to the *idea* of letters and their sounds. You can help familiarise him with this concept in the following way. Move your finger slowly under a word and say the sound of each individual letter. Do this again and then read the word at normal speed. Only do this with words that have fairly regular sound patterns such as hat, dog, rug, box. Avoid words like chair, sheep, there, where the individual letters do not have their true sounds.

You can also start drawing his attention to a particular letter sound, perhaps the first letter of his name. See if your child can pick it out in words. Try at the beginnings of words first and then the ends. If he is interested in this he might be ready to play some of the Sound Games on page 70.

55

The following games will increase your child's range of Look and Say words. Check your collection of cut-outs to see that you have a good selection of clearly illustrated objects that will fit onto cards 4″ × 3″ (10 × 7½ cm). Choose the objects that will most interest your child—one of the great advantages of a home-made scheme is that it can be tailor made to appeal to each child by basing it on his particular interests.

Extending Look and Say Vocabulary

WORD AND PICTURE CARDS

You will need
Cards, about 4″ × 3″ (10 × 7½ cm)
Felt pen
Cut-outs (see page 44)
Glue

Aims—to increase the child's Look and Say vocabulary; to maintain his interest by varying the approach used in name and word cards.

Method

1. Stick or draw pictures onto cards and for every picture make a separate word card.
2. Show the child one of the pictures and talk about it. Then show him the corresponding word card.
3. Run your finger under the word, saying it slowly; encourage him to do the same and place the two cards together.
4. It will depend on the child's span of concentration or interest whether you introduce the next pair of cards at the same or a later session. It will be helpful if the first two words have markedly different word shapes (page 18).
5. When your child is familiar with the two pairs of cards lay them face upwards and pick out one of the word cards, saying, 'This card says **sun**. Can you put its picture next to it?'
6. When he has done this pick out the remaining picture and ask him to put its word beside it.
7. This has been very easy so far. Next time select the picture first.
8. Add new words only when the child has mastered the existing ones.

Your child will probably enjoy pairing the words and pictures on his own. Always check his efforts and give him lots of praise and encouragement.

Word and Picture Games

PARTNERS

1. Spread some cards face up before you.
2. Pick up one of the pictures and give it to the child.
3. He finds the word that goes with it. If he is right he keeps the pair of cards.
4. He then picks out a picture for you to find its corresponding word.
5. Continue until there are no more cards.

HUNT THE PARTNER

1. Spread the cards face downwards on the table.
2. Pick up one card at random, and place it face up on the table.
3. Each turn up a card—replacing it face down—until one of you finds the partner.
4. Whoever finds the partner keeps the pair of cards.
5. The winner then turns up a new card and has the first go at looking for its partner.
6. The winner of the game is the one with the most pairs.

   This game is also a useful exercise in memory training as it pays to remember which cards you have picked up and what was on them. Try and help your child to do this. You may find he quickly learns to beat you!

LOTTO

1. You each have an equal number of picture cards turned upwards before you.
2. Shuffle the pile of corresponding word cards and place them face down.
3. Turn up one word at a time. Whoever has the right picture claims the word card and places it on top of that picture card. The winner is the first one to cover all his picture cards.

WORD AND PICTURE SNAP

1. Sort the cards into two piles: words in one, pictures in the other.
2. Turn the piles face down.
3. Each take a pile and turn over your cards in turn. When a picture and its matching word card are showing at the same time the first to call out the word wins a counter or button.
4. When you come to the bottom of the piles turn them over, cut and start again. The winner is the one with most counters.

WHO'S HIDING HERE?

This game requires only the word and picture cards and can be easy or difficult according to the age and ability of the child. Even very young children will enjoy this in its simplest form. For the simplest version you will need two or three picture cards. Sit *beside* the child.

1. Place the cards picture side up in a line from left to right. Point to each card in turn and ask the child to name the picture.
2. Turn the cards face down.
3. Starting on the left, point to the card and ask the child: 'Who's hiding here?'
4. When he has told you, let him turn the cards over to see if he is right.

   Later, when he has had more experience

matching picture and word cards, you can introduce word cards into the game. At stage 3, when you ask 'Who's hiding here?', instead of giving you a verbal answer the child can pick out the appropriate word card and place it on the picture card.

PICTURE HOP SCOTCH

This is a little more challenging than the previous word and picture games and should only be played when your child has mastered these comfortably. In addition to reading the word cards he must be able to count to six and 'read' a dice.

You will need
   12 picture cards and corresponding word cards
   1 dice and shaker

Method
1. Each take 6 picture cards and line them up in front of you. Place the word cards face up in random order where they can be read easily.
2. The first player throws the dice. If, for example, he throws a 4 he counts to the fourth card, the card nearest to him being 1. He finds the relevant word card and covers the fourth picture with it.
3. The dice passes to the next player.
   When a number is thrown for a card that is already covered the player cannot move for that turn. The winner is the one who covers all his cards first.
   It can take many throws to get the right numbers to cover the last few cards. The element of chance makes this an exciting game.
   This game can be extended to appeal to older children by using 24 pairs of word and picture cards and 2 dice.

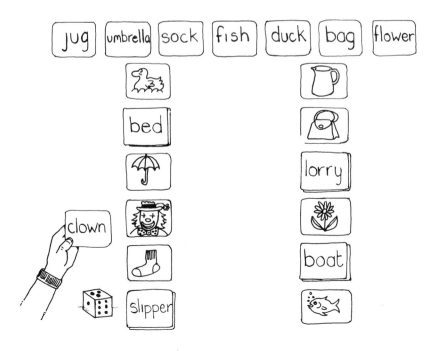

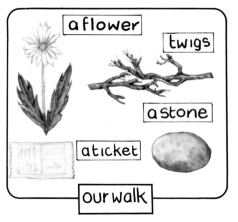

our walk

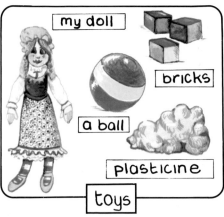

toys

things we eat

MUSEUM

If you take your child to a museum or exhibition, you may be able to enthuse him with the idea of having his own museum corner.

The exhibits can be simple everyday objects and should be clearly labelled. Find a place at child's height where they can be set out for a few days— you may have to turn a blind eye to having your windowsill or coffee table covered in twigs and stones!

Make a word card for each exhibit. Look at them together and ask the child to put them in their right places.

Just leaving the exhibits and cards standing is not necessarily going to make the child look at the words. He needs to practise using them. Why not cast yourself in the role of Mrs Muddle, a curator's nightmare, who keeps dusting the objects and disorganising their labels? The child has to sort them out again. Give him the chance to play Mr or Mrs Muddle to your long-suffering museum attendant.

If it would be more convenient for the cards to stand up, cut the card to twice the required depth and fold across the middle.

Colour Words

Make word cards for some of the colours —**red blue yellow green orange.**

If help is needed, lightly stick a piece of coloured paper on to the back of the card so that it can be removed later. Teach the cards one by one allowing the child to peep at the colour when he needs to. Let him practise them in this way: Say to the child 'Show me something . . .' holding up a colour word. The child points out something that colour.

Alternatively you could play this with a box of coloured crayons, the child picking up the appropriate crayon.

Matching

Write the names of different colours on separate sheets of paper. Give the child some crayons or gummed shapes and ask him to draw or stick each colour with its word. Pin the results on the wall.

RAINBOW RACE

More active children will probably enjoy this game. Several children can play, but make sure you have a colour item for each child or it might end in tears or quarrels.

You will need

Cards with colour words written on and corresponding coloured objects (bricks, toys, etc.).

Method

1. Line the objects up at one end of the room. Talk about rainbows as you do this, Has he seen one for real or in a book? When do you see rainbows? What colours are in them? (If he knows nothing at all about rainbows then ignore these suggestions.)
2. You and the child go to the other end of the room with the cards. You say to him: 'Run to the rainbow and fetch me something . . .' (holding up a word card).
3. He runs and brings you the right coloured article.

To adapt the game for pre-reading children, instead of writing words, paint a colour on each card. Lay out the objects as above and ask the child to 'Run to the rainbow and fetch me something the same colour as this' (holding up the colour).

Action Words

So far, your child has learned words for people and objects. The games on these two pages will introduce him to action words and will appeal to the active child. Before making any action cards, check on what action words your child understands. Give him some instructions and see if he can carry them out.

hop to the table
run to the door

As always it is preferable if the child has come across these words in a sentence before he learns them in isolation.

Write some captions such as

baby can crawl

and encourage him to draw pictures for them.

Make word cards for actions such as

run skip hop walk jump sit crawl stop

If necessary provide pin-men picture clues that can be cut off later. But make sure that the child understands the drawing; hopping can easily be mistaken for jumping, or walking for running. As with all the previous words, introduce them gradually.

Action Games

THE CARD SAYS

Say to your child 'The card says . . .' and hold up one of the action words. He performs the action written on the card. If he is right he keeps the card if not it goes back in your pile and he tries it later. Provided you have the stamina let him have a turn at holding the cards up for you to do the actions. Keep him on his toes by occasionally doing the wrong action and letting him put you right.

HUNT THE CARD

Hide the cards separately in a room or garden. When the child finds a card he does the action written on it until you check that he is right. He continues searching until all the cards are found.

MUSICAL ACTIONS

Place the cards on the floor around the room. Turn on some music or sing, and walk around the room until the music stops. Then run to the nearest card and do the action written on it until the music starts again.

THE RUNNING–JUMPING–STANDING STILL RACE

More than one player is needed for this game so if there are no other children available you will have to take an active part yourself.

You will need
   Action cards
   Space for racing

Method
1. Lay out the course by spacing the cards on the ground or floor between the starting and finishing point.
2. At the starting signal the players read the first card. If it says **jump** they jump to the next card. If this one says **crawl** they crawl to the next card and so on to the end.
3. After each race re-arrange the cards so the players cannot depend on remembering the previous race.
   You can either remove the inactive words like stop and sit, or agree to stop or sit and count to a particular number or sing a song before moving on to the next card.

THE GREASEPROOF PAPER GAME

This game continues to extend your child's repertoire of Look and Say words. It has an in-built self-correcting device enabling the child to check his own answer. This will help a hesitant child feel more confident.

Your child will feel more involved in this game if you lead into it via a recently enjoyed activity such as shopping, making jam tarts or a special outing. Chat about the event and draw some of the things that you discuss.

You may find that the drawing and chatting are all that can be managed in one session. Add the words later.

You will need

Large sheet of plain card or paper at least 2 feet (60 cm) square
Felt pen
Some greaseproof rectangles 2" × 4" 5 × 10 cm).
Gummed dots or other gummed shapes

Aims—to learn more Look and Say words, the self-correcting device enabling the child to learn more independently; to encourage the child to look at words and make simple discriminations between them; to look at words from left to right.

Method

1. Onto the card or paper draw three or four objects (if you are unhappy about drawing use your cut-outs).
2. Discuss the objects and write the name of each under it (the word should not be larger than the greaseproof rectangle).
3. Make sure that the child understands the connection between the picture and the word.
4. Place a greaseproof rectangle over each word and trace over it.
5. Stick a gummed dot under the first letter of each greaseproof word. This acts as a guide indicating the right side of the paper.
6. Show how the greaseproof word fits over its matching word on the card.
7. Give the child one traced word at a time to place on its matching partner on the card.

After playing, clip the greaseproof words onto the card or place them in an envelope which could be glued onto a corner of the card.

This game is self-correcting: if the greaseproof word does not exactly cover the one below, the child can tell for himself that it is not the same word.

When you start this game bear in mind the section of Word Shapes (page 18)

and do not choose words that are similar in shape.

The next time you play this game add one or two more objects to the card but do not overcrowd it. Make up new cards to cover other topics of interest.

If the child has any difficulty in matching the words you can help in the following way. Cut some longer greaseproof strips 2" × 8" (5 × 20 cm) and draw the object on one half of the strip as a clue; the drawing can be cut off later.

Putting Words Together

By now your child can read many useful words. But he has mainly experienced them as isolated words and has had little practice reading them in the context of a phrase or a short sentence although he will have *heard* you using them in sentences.

Reading is more than the sum total of recognising individual words. Firstly, it is knowing the order in which to look at words—left to right along the lines, top to bottom of the page. Secondly, it is understanding the whole sense of the combined words, often referred to as *reading for meaning*.

In the Hide and Seek Game (page 53) your child experienced the left to right of reading and reading for meaning when he followed the phrase and sentence clues. Since then he has increased his stock of reading words by playing the games and it is now time to consolidate this by practising these new words in context. Start thinking of possible ways of combining them into meaningful groups. You will increase your scope if you first teach the three words: **a, big** and **little**.

Show your child what happens when you put **a** in front of other words; how **tree** becomes **a tree, window** becomes **a window**. Let him try it in front of other words himself (you must pre-select the suitable cards).

Make a word card for **big** and one for **little**. Assemble several pairs of objects of contrasting sizes, such as a little shoe and a big shoe, a little spoon and a big spoon. Discuss these objects and their sizes and show the child the cards. Practise putting the **big** and **little** cards against the appropriate objects in each pair. Make sure he can tell the difference easily.

Word Groups

Now look through your notebook or envelope of word cards and see how you can combine some of the words that your child already knows?
a yellow car
a blue ball
a big house
a little box
mummy is on the chair
the cup is on the table
Here are two ways in which you can practise word groups. Choose whichever suits you better.

1. Lay out the word card to make a short phrase as above. Help the child to read it. Ask him to draw what is written on the cards and, under his drawing, write the phrase. This accustoms him to recognising familiar words in a context and so increases his reading experience. Pin the drawing on the wall, or, if he has several, you might staple them together to make a book.

2. Write out some word groups on strips of paper or card about $10'' \times 2''$ (25×5 cm) and make an appropriate picture card to illustrate each strip. Help your child to read a strip and see if he can select the right picture card to put beside it.

A more difficult exercise is to get the child himself to arrange words into phrases and sentences. Pre-select the cards that you will need (no more than ten to start with) and lay them face up in front of the child. First of all ask him to pick out the cards for say, **a house**, and place them together. Encourage him to read his two words to you, pointing at each one. Once he can manage two-word combinations try three-word groups and so on until he can put a simple sentence together.

Key Words

So far in the games we have neglected a very important group of words and their absence is felt once you start making up phrases and sentences. These are the small connecting words that appear with the greatest frequency in spoken and written vocabulary. (See the Key Words chart on page 19.)

WINDOW STRIPS

You will need
Piece of card (or sturdy paper) about 15″ (40 cm) square, (larger if it is to be used with a group of children.
Strips of card (or sturdy paper) $\frac{1}{2}$″ (1 cm) longer than the square and $1\frac{1}{2}$″ (4 cm) deep
Craft knife

Write simple phrases on the strips. Draw a picture at the other end. Cut slots in the card.

Aims—to familiarise the child with reading word groups; reading Key Words; left-to-right and top-to-bottom direction of reading.

Method
1. Insert the strips so that the writing shows but the picture is hidden.
2. The child reads the first phrase, then pulls the strip along so the illustration appears in the picture window.
3. He does the same with the next phrase and so on.
   Make several sets of strips based on members of the family or particular events. Using the same basic chart you can change the story every day. When you introduce a new word, use it several times to help 'fix' it in the child's mind.

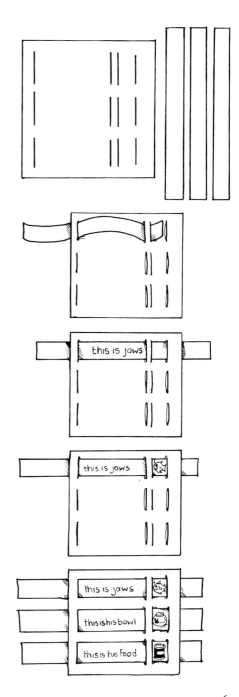

Phonic Games

In his Look and Say games, your child has learned to read words without knowing either the sound or the appearance of the individual letters. He has been dependent on you to tell him every new word and dependent on the games for the repetition necessary to memorise the words.

In the Phonic games, he will learn how a spoken word is composed of individual sounds blended together and that each of these sounds is represented by letters which are combined to make the written word. This knowledge will provide the tools that will enable him eventually to decode new words and hence achieve reading independence.

Dovetailing Look and Say and Phonics
There should not be a sudden switch from the Look and Say approach to Phonic games but rather a shift in emphasis. If you followed the suggestions in Looking Ahead (page 55) you have already made a tentative start on sounds. Continue playing the Look and Say games but begin using the word cards

to back up the teaching of sounds and letters. The more you can relate new information to whatever is already familiar, the more firmly will the child grasp new ideas and knowledge.

Sounds

Remember; use the *sounds* of letters and not their names (page 17).

The first step in the Phonic games is to begin training the child's ear to distinguish the groups of sounds that make up a spoken word. At the moment your child probably hears the word **cat** as a single sound. With your help he can learn to notice that it is made up of separate sounds blended together.
The idea that a spoken word is the result of blending together separate sounds is so familiar to an adult that it is easy to forget that a child has to learn this.

If you have listened to an unfamiliar language you will know how it appears to flow in an unbroken stream of sound in which you cannot recognise where one word ends and the next begins. Although your child can generally recognise separate words, he may need a lot of help in distinguishing individual sounds.

Remember that he may not be physically mature enough to develop this skill. In this case, you must bide your time and provide opportunities for developing *auditory discrimination* by listening in a light-hearted way to sounds, rhymes and words. Begin drawing attention to a particular letter sound —perhaps the initial sound of his name. Say aloud other words beginning with this sound. Can the child tell you what sound they begin with? Can *he* think of words beginning with this sound? Once he can do this try him on I Spy and Odd-One-Out on page 70.

Alphabet books

A well illustrated alphabet book can link both the teaching of letter sounds and letter shapes. Make sure that the letters are written in lower case. There may be capitals as well, but reject a book that has *only* capitals.

The picture below is a page from an a b c book called the First Book of Sounds published by Macdonald Educational. A book like this would be useful for the older pre-school child who has become bored with very simple a b c books.

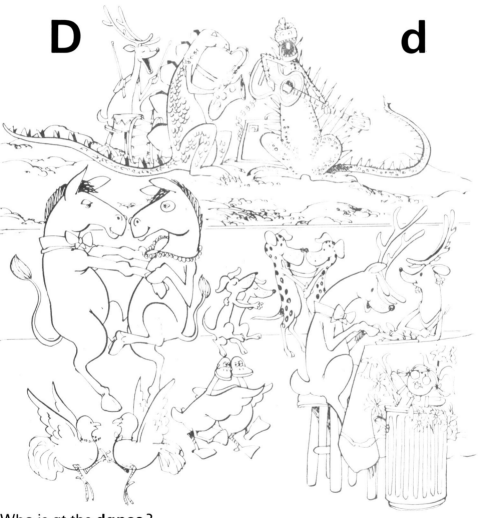

D   d

Who is at the **dance**?

Do you know the names of these animals?

They all start with **d**.

I-SPY

This familiar game provides practice in listening to letter sounds. For a small child the usual formula of 'I spy with my little eye something beginning with. with . . .' can be too difficult. You may have to give help such as 'I spy with my little eye something that we put on our feet when it rains and begins with b. . . .'

As has already been mentioned the physical ability to hear the difference between sounds may not have developed yet and your child may find these exercises difficult. Or he may experience difficulty with only certain sounds that are similar such as **b** and **p**, or **r** and **w**. Unless you think there is a hearing problem, in which case, do seek medical advice, *time* will solve these difficulties.

Play about with sounds. Make up rhythms using the sound of a letter:
b-b-b.b.b.
and ask the child to repeat it to you. Sing nursery rhymes replacing the words with a letter.

Tongue twisters are a jolly way of making a child aware of the initial sounds of words.

cat

hat

tap

ODD-ONE-OUT

Say four or five words which all begin with the same letter except for one:
carrot carpet cup donkey cake pepperpot bicycle pineapple paper pan
The child has to pick out the odd word.

Final letters
In due course the last letter of a word should be recognised and you can play odd-one-out in the same way.
e.g. **cat bat hat can**

The Shapes of Letters

In addition to learning that **cat** is made up of separate sounds, the child eventually has to learn that each of these sounds is represented by a symbol or written letter, and that these letters are put together in a particular order to make the word that he recognises as **cat**. Just grasping this idea requires a considerable mental leap, quite apart from learning 26 letters and linking them with their sounds—so go very slowly.

She sells seashells on the seashore.

Letter Cards

Teach only one letter at a time and do not go on to a new letter until your child is confident with the previous one.

Cut some cards about $2\frac{1}{2}'' \times 4''$ (6 × 10 cm). On the left-hand side write the letter clearly and on the right-hand side draw something or stick a cut-out to illustrate the letter at the beginning of a word.

The illustration beside the letter is an aid that can eventually be dispensed with but to start with use it as the clue to what the letter is. When he says 'dog', ask him what sound 'dog' begins with. You then draw his attention to the letter on the card telling him that this letter is **d** (duh). Ask the child to think of other things that begin with **d**. In this or a future session start a letter corner as suggested on the next page. Go slowly, especially in the early stages when the child is absorbing the *idea* of letters generally as well as the individual information about each one.

When you think that he knows the letter without the aid of the drawing, you can either fold the drawing back to act as an occasional point of reference, cut it off, or make plain letter cards.

When letter cards have been thoroughly learned, try turning them into simple two-piece jigsaws by cutting between each letter and picture.

Letter Order

Do not teach letters in alphabetical order, as this bears no relevance to the frequency with which they are used.

There is no need to become a slave to a list and it is a good idea to build on anything that has a personal significance. You might find that a good starting point is the first letter of the child's name, or perhaps there is a particular initial letter which appears frequently on your word cards.

Do not use as examples words in which the initial letter does not make its usual sound, as in **giraffe** or **Cinderella**, or where it is blended with another letter as in **chip, thimble** or **shop**.

Avoid teaching letters of similar shape (**b** and **d**, **p** and **q**, **n** and **u**, **c** and **e**) too close together. Allow a lapse of time and several intervening letters between similar shapes. Include some vowels amongst your early letters to prepare for the Word Building games (page 78).

LETTER CORNER

To help a child link a written letter
with its sound have a letter corner.
Find a surface that the child can reach
—a small table, low shelf, corner of his
bedroom floor—and place a letter card
on it. Together, find as many items as
you can that begin with the letter and
place them in the letter corner.

Your child will probably start with
simple letter sounds such as **m** for
mouse. Later he may notice that
blended sounds such as **sp** for **spade** and
sn for **snake** both begin with the same
letter.

LETTER SCRAP BOOK

Buy or make a scrap book. Each time
you introduce a new letter write it at
the top of a page. Go through your
cut-outs and help the child to pick out the
ones that begin with that letter and stick
them on to the page. Write the word
under each cut-out and not at random or
it could be confusing as the picture above
shows.

Capital Letters

You can use the scrap book or wall
charts to introduce capital letters.
Once the child has fixed the lower-case
letter in his mind you can write its
capital alongside it as the need arises.
Explain to him that, sometimes, when
a letter is at the beginning of a special
word, like someone's name, it likes to
look more important. Refer to capital
letters as 'big letters' and lower-case
letters as 'little letters'.

Playing the Letter Games

Learning letters may require a lot of
time and repetition which could become a
chore unless you keep things interesting
by varying the approach. The following
games provide different ways to practise
the same two skills.

● Recognising initial sounds of words.
● Linking sounds with written letters.

You may not need to work through
every game. Choose the ones that suit you.

Look at Word Building on page 75
once your child has a good working
knowledge of a dozen or so letters.

SHOPPING WITH LETTERS

You will need
  Letter cards
  A good imagination

Method
1. The child is the shopkeeper with the letters in front of him.
2. You are his chatting customer. Your conversation may go something like this, 'Now, I've got to make a cake so I'd better have some flour. Have you got **f** for flour? And I think I've run out of margarine so can I have **m** for margarine.' Don't forget to pronounce letter *sounds*, not names.
3. The child gives you the letters as you ask for them.
   When he is proficient at picking out the beginnings of words himself you will not need to ask for the letter, he will work that out for himself. The child then has a turn at being the shopper.
   For a more sophisticated version of this game you can place some objects on the table for the shopper to buy. The shopper then has the letters and 'pays' the shopkeeper with the appropriate letter for each item that he buys.

THINGUMMY BAG

You will need
  Bag
  Several objects, e.g. pencil, spoon, book, hat
  Letter card for the initial of each item, e.g. **p, s, b, h.**

Method
1. Put the objects in the bag.
2. The child spreads the letter cards in front of him saying the sound of each.
3. He dips into the bag, brings out an object and places it next to its appropriate letter.

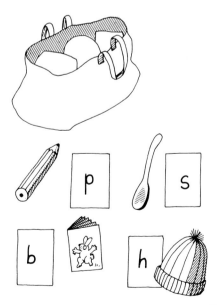

LETTER BOX

Once you have made the letter box, this game can be played in any odd moment and is one that the child should eventually be able to enjoy on his own. Making the box, requires more preparation than most of the other games, but you should find it worth it in the long run.

You will need
Clean envelopes
Sturdy cardboard grocery box about 2 feet (60 cm) high
Picture cards that fit into the envelopes (your previous cards should do—it does not matter if they stand higher than the envelopes).

Aim—to give practice in recognising the initial sounds of words and linking them with their written letters.

To make
1. Turn the grocery box bottom up (cover or paint if you wish).
2. Seal the evelopes and then slit them open with a sharp knife—this turns them into pockets.
3. After writing a lower case letter clearly on each envelope, stick them on to the box. (You may start with just a few envelopes and add to the box as the child learns more letters.)
4. Sort out a collection of picture cards whose initial sounds correspond to the letters on the envelopes.

To play
1. Go over the letters with the child encouraging him to say their sounds and think of words beginning with the sounds.
2. Give him a picture card and ask him what it is.

3. Ask what sound that word begins with.
4. He finds the appropriate letter envelope and posts the card into it.
    Always go over his efforts when he has been sorting on his own. The upturned bottom of the box makes a useful surface on which he can lay out his cards.

SPIN A LETTER

You will need
8 picture cards
A cardboard disc (the size of a yoghourt carton).
Draw 8 sections on the disc and write a letter corresponding to each of your picture cards in each section.
Pierce the centre with a match, cocktail stick or sharp pencil on which the disc can spin.

Method
1. Share out the picture cards.
2. Spin the disc.

Spin a Letter

Letter Skittles

3. When it comes to rest on a letter, whoever has the appropriate picture card surrenders it.
4. The winner is the one who gets rid of all his cards first.

LETTER SKITTLES

You will need
Some improvised skittles (3 or 4 plastic squash bottles or cardboard tubes).
Soft ball
Different letter card for each skittle.

Method
1. Attach a letter card to each skittle and line them up.
2. Players take it in turns to knock down a skittle with the ball. When a player gets one down he must think of a word that begins that that letter. So if it is **m** he could call out '**m** is for **man**'. He cannot have a word that has been called before and if he does he must miss a turn.

Word Building

Two-letter words
Once your child is familiar with some letters and their sounds (including some vowels), you can begin to make two-letter words with him. Depending on the letters he already knows, try any of these words:
am at if in on up us
At this stage avoid words where the letters are not true to their proper sounds. In the word **as**, for example, the **s** is hard and pronounced **z**. The **f** of **of** is also hard and pronounced **v**.

When you have decided on your word, place the two letter cards together. Point to them in turn asking the child to sound each letter. After doing this several times, he may be able to tell you the whole word. If not then you point to the letters saying their individual sounds yourself and then running them together into a whole word. If he cannot grasp the idea, do not make a chore of it, just tell him the word. Come back to it another time and go through the routine again. Perhaps he will tell you then!

Keep playing about with two-letter words until the child can blend them effortlessly into whole words. This may take a few days, weeks or months. If there is any difficulty do not dwell too long on the activity—just touch upon it lightly between other games until it clicks.

When your child can manage this, see if he can place two letters together to make a word himself.

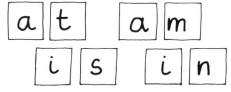

75

Three-letter Words

When your child can work out two-letter words try putting some three-letter words together with him. Let these incorporate your two-letter combinations to enable him to work with familiar material. For example, if he can read **at**, try

cat hat mat fat rat.

He should get the idea if you lay out the cards for **rat** and, when he has read that to you, or you have told him, substitute the **r** for **m** to make **mat** and so on.

This activity must be handled very cautiously. If you dwell on it too long the child may quickly become bored. Young children may also not be sufficiently mature to distinguish sounds precisely and you may have to be very patient and wait until they have this ability.

When he can read these words comfortably, try the following exercise.

Taking off the last letter

When he has read a word, remove its last letter and ask him to tell you the sound that is left. For example, if the words were **mat, bit, peg**, can he now say **ma-, bi-,** and **pe-** as whole sounds (not as individual letters). When he can do this, extend his word building repertoire by adding letters to the ends of these pairs of letters.

ma can become **man, mac** or **map**
bi can become **bin, big** or **bib**
pe can become **peg, pen** or **pet**.

Some other combinations are suggested below but there are many other possibilities:

ra—g—m—n—t
ha—d—m—s—t
po—d—p—t
bu—d—g—n—s—t
ca—n—p—t
pi—g—n—p

When he becomes familiar with the construction of words, ask your child if he can do some 'letter magic' and change **mat** into **man**, or **pig** into **pin** using the letter cards himself.

In these word building exercises you have followed this sequence:
1. Building two-letter words.
2. Adding a letter to make three-letter words.
3. Changing a letter to make new words.

Each step has arisen from the step before so that the child has always built on to an existing framework of information and has not been required to make any great leaps into the unfamiliar. He has always practised blending sounds and letters in the context of a word. He has not had to do any exercises blending meaningless sounds.

Making Words

Help your child to arrange letter cards to make some words himself. To start with you might give him three letters that make a familiar word and help him to put them in the right order. This involves him in arranging the letters in sequence but not in selecting them.

When he can manage to arrange them, try mixing the three cards amongst some others so that he must select his letters as well as arranging them. Talk him through these word-building activities to encourage him to develop a logical approach.

This may be similar to the kind of approach you use when you show your child how to assemble a construction toy. By understanding how the pieces relate to each other he is learning how to make the construction himself.

When Words Misbehave

A child who enjoys constructing words, or an older child who is beginning to write, will soon discover that not all words are written as they sound. A child making the word **badge** for example, may use his knowledge of letters and sounds and produce **baj**. This would show a very intelligent application and knowledge of letters and sounds but of course it is wrong. In a case like this you would have to make it clear to the child that he has worked the word out very well, but that some words are 'a bit naughty' and do not always behave as we expect. There is no need to go into long explanations or make a problem of it—just make a word card so that it can be learned by sight as a Look and Say word.

Good Friends ck sh th st ch

Some letter combinations like **ck** and **sh** are very common and can be introduced as the need arises. A particular combination may crop up frequently in new words and you might draw attention to it; or a child may need to use it himself when word building. If, for example, he makes the word **sock** as **soc** or **sok** by applying his knowledge of sounds and

letters, you can use the opportunity to tell him that **c** and **k** are good friends who like to go around together. Point out other examples of **ck** in familiar words. Make a word card for **sock** and a letter card for **ck**. Over the next few sessions reinforce the information by drawing his attention to other **ck** words such as

> **back sack neck peck lick kick**
> **tick pick sick rock cock luck**

Any of the letter pairs can be taught like this, but remember to treat each pair as a single entity.

Word Building Cards

These cards will be superfluous if the child can manage word building with great ease but if he needs some practice they will provide a welcome variation. If you use them to help him learn the letter combinations **st sh ck th** then be sure to treat these like a single letter, keeping them together.

Make whichever of the two kinds of cards suits you best—they give the child the same practice. If you are dependent on cut-outs the square one will give you more scope for larger illustrations but if you can draw your own pictures the long ones are easier to make.

You can simply let the child match the cards—encourage him to say the first two letters as a whole sound **ha, su, cu** etc. and to say the complete word when he adds the last letter.

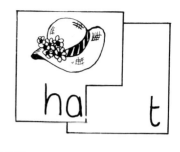

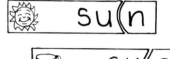

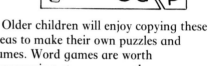

Older children will enjoy copying these ideas to make their own puzzles and games. Word games are worth encouraging at any age as they are an excellent way of helping children to increase their vocabulary and improve their spelling.

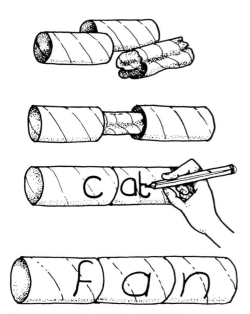

ROTATING LOO ROLLS

You can give further practice in word building using loo rolls or any other cardboard tubes.

Method
1. Take three rolls and slightly squash one so that it will just wedge into the other rolls. Fit the unsquashed rolls over either end of the squashed one to meet in the middle.
2. Write initial letters on one roll and the rest of some words on the other.
3. The child rotates the rolls to make different words.

Variation
1. Using a craft knife cut a roll into three portions and fit them over a squashed roll.
2. Write vowels on the middle section and consonants on the outside, to allow easy words to be made.
3. The child rotates the letters to see how many words he can make.

WINDOWS

You will need
Piece of card about 6″ × 2½″
(15 × 6 cm).
Some card strips—see diagram
Felt pen
Craft knife for making the slits.
Make the card as shown in the diagram. You are not likely to find cut-outs small enough for the windows so have a shot at drawing the things you want. Let your child see you do the drawing and discuss them with him.

Method
The child slides a drawing into the first window and slides the right letter into the last window to make the correct word.

Where there are letter combinations such as **ck sh th** at the end of a word, be sure not to separate them. Make **ve-st fi-sh** or **ba-ck**.

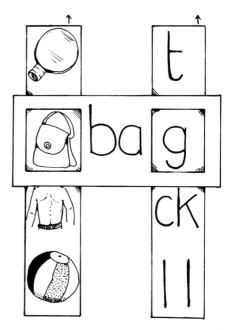

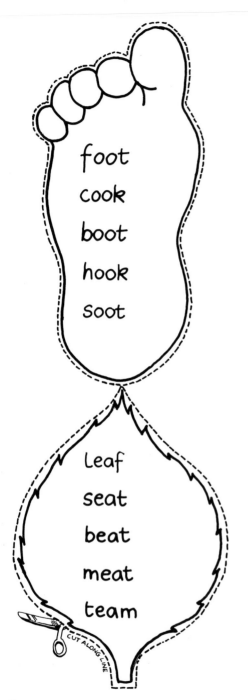

foot

cook

boot

hook

soot

Leaf

seat

beat

meat

team

CUT ALONG LINE

Vowel Blends

Certain vowel combinations or 'blends'
occur fairly frequently—**ee ea oo
ai oa**. When a child encounters these
in words such as
seed bean look out rain goat
he may have difficulty in working them
out from his knowledge of individual
letter sounds.

It is not suggested that you teach
these blends in isolation but that you
are aware of them and handle them as
they occur in the natural course of
events. Some of them have probably
appeared already in the Look and Say
words. Look back over the word cards
and make a note of these. They will be
useful as examples.

When you teach a blend you can give
it interest and impact in the following
way. Cut out an appropriately shaped
piece of card or paper. For example,
for **oo** cut out a large foot, for **ea** cut
out a large leaf, and write words with this
blend on to the shape. Pin them up in a
prominent place and go over them
together from time to time.

Making Books

In the pre-reading activities and the
reading games it has been suggested
that you make books with your child.
This enables you to create something
based on his own life and interests
which will therefore have a great personal
appeal for him. It is better if the book
uses the child's own drawings and ideas.
For by giving recognition to his own work
in this way you help to increase his
self-respect and confidence. It also helps
him to feel more at home with books.

Now that his reading vocabulary is
fairly large see if you can guide him into

making up a story for a book. You write the story as he tells it and he does the pictures. It need only be a few pages long but it is sufficient that it is his own.

In order that your child can feel pleased and proud of his book you must be prepared to take a little trouble making it. Packets of play paper or typing paper make cheap pages and save you the problem of cutting them to the same size. The pages can be stitched together, stapled, held in a plastic binder (but they don't open flat with these) or punched and threaded with wool or metal clip rings.

Put the book title and the child's name on the front page and, for your own interest, write the date.

He will probably enjoy returning to these again and again and because the words are his own he is more likely to remember them and hence learn to read them.

Shape books
These make an interesting variation or addition to the shape cards. They will particularly appeal to a child who enjoys drawing. Stitch some pages together and cut the book to an appropriate shape.

Clean the
rabbit hutch
after tea.

Reading in Action

From playing the Look and Say and Phonic games your child can now recognise many words on sight and decode unfamiliar but simple words using his knowledge of letters and their sounds. He has practised using individual words and letters in his games and also knows how to read a group of words. It is now time to bring reading into the context of everyday life in ways that are interesting and exciting. With this in mind try out any of these suggestions that you think will capture your child's interest and imagination.

Memos

If you have promised to do something for the child later in the day or want to remind yourselves of something, write out a memo. Write clearly on a large sheet of paper or card with a drawing by yourself or the child to illustrate the message. Let the child see you write it and be sure that he understands what it says. Then ask him to put it in a prominent place where you can both see it and ask him to read it to you occasionally during the day. If you hope to convey the idea that writing is a useful means of communication you must be conscientious about following up your memos.

If this is successful keep the memos in a box for him to get out and look back at, or staple them together to make a book. Because these have a personal importance for him he is likely to remember the messages.

If you can, try and include several familiar words in each message but where you have to use a new word look for an opportunity to use it again soon. This will help to 'fix' it in his mind.

Dear Jo,
Daddy is on
holiday tomorrow.
We will all go
swimming.
Love from
Mummy
X

Letters

We all like to receive letters, so how about doing a simple letter—a drawing and a sentence—for your child. Try and make the drawing illustrate the message as clearly as possible to help him work out any unfamiliar words.

You might leave the letter beside his bed at night or give it to him when you receive your morning post.

In His Own Words

Now that he has a large selection of word cards a child can start arranging them to make his own simple sentences. You may find it necessary at this stage to re-make the word cards on a smaller scale as a child may find it hard to scan across a large area.

Store the words so that they can all be seen at the same time. Tape some strips of card horizontally in rows on a stiff sheet of card to form long pockets. Tuck the words into the pockets so that they are all visible at a glance.

When a child has arranged his words into a sentence, copy them out for him into a book.

TREASURE HUNT

This is a slightly more complicated version of the Hide and Seek game on page 53. Make some clue cards suitable for using in a particular room such as: **behind the sofa, under the rug, in the cupboard.** The child goes out of the room whilst you hide the object—bear this game in mind when you have a small treat to give him. Then hide the object and in another part of the room place a card indicating the whereabouts of the object. Somewhere else, you place a card indicating the whereabouts of the previous card. Got it? Sounds complicated but it isn't really!

When the child comes into the room you give him the first clue card to set him off on the trail.

WEATHER CHART AND PICTURE BOARD

If you have a pin board or blackboard make a space on it. Or else find a convenient patch of wall or a little-used cupboard door where you can pin up word cards.

Make a word card for every day of the week enlisting the child's help. 'What day comes after Monday? Now let me see what letter does that begin with?'

Then make cards for different weather conditions
sunny, cloudy, rain, windy
and ask the child to do drawings above the writing.

Put the cards in an envelope and store them on the board. Try and establish a regular time in the daily routine when you do the weather chart.

Keep a space by the chart where the child can put his picture for every day. Perhaps the child (or you if he is not in the mood) could do a picture of something that has happened in the day with a short caption underneath.

If you store them on a bulldog clip you will have a ready-made book for him to look at.

DIARY SCRAP BOOK

It is particularly interesting to make one of these at holiday times. Everyone in the family makes a contribution each day in the form of a drawing, a sentence or some souvenir, entrance ticket or post card.

You will find that you get as much pleasure as the children in looking over these and reading them again a long time afterwards.

84

The First Reader

So far, you have been reading books regularly to your child. He has enjoyed playing the reading games and from these he can recognise a good number of words by the Look and Say method and can de-code fairly simple words using his knowledge of letters and sounds. He should be able to read, with some understanding, phrases and sentences that contain familiar words. He may also be able to make an intelligent guess at new words where there is a picture or a sentence context to help him. He may enjoy reading sentences from familiar story books.

Sometimes he may try 'pretend' reading or reciting a story from memory. You may be able to harness this enthusiasm by tactfully guiding him through the left-to-right direction of reading and helping him with words. But do be cautious, he may not always welcome your intrusion.

The important thing is that he should feel confident with books. They should feel like good friends. As his reading skills develop he is going to want books that are at a suitable level for reading by himself with minimum assistance from you. So the next question to consider is how to set about choosing the most suitable books.

Many bookshops encourage young readers by holding story-telling sessions. Joan Dashwood (left) invited Michael Bond (centre) and Brian Rawlinson (right) to meet children at the Rainbow Bookshop, Walton-on-Thames.

85

How to choose a first reading book

When selecting a first reader bear the following points in mind.

● Is the story/subject matter likely to hold his interest?

● Are the illustrations clear and interesting and do they depict what is going on in the story? Remember that the pictures will provide clues to unfamiliar words.

● There should be no more than 10 or 12 words to each page and preferably less for the very first book.

● Does the story use the kind of words that your child understands?

● Is the print clear, not too small and in lower-case? Take special notice of the gs and as. They should be written as here and *not* **g** or **a**.

● Is the printing well laid out with a clear space around the words and not jumbled on the page?

● Is the vocabulary *controlled*—is there an attempt to reinforce words by repeating them?

You may be able to incorporate some of the words from the book into your games to reinforce your child's experience of them.

If you can, it is worth arming yourself with several books because once the child gets the taste for reading his own book he is going to want to move on to another—and another. This may seem a little extravagant but there are plenty of well-produced cheap paperback readers and no other toy or treat is going to have quite the same long-term impact as his first readers. Your child might enjoy helping you to choose them.

Heffer's Bookshops, Cambridge, prepares for an invasion of children to meet Raymond Briggs at a Christmas story-telling session.

When you have chosen your books, go through one together looking at the pictures and talking about them. You may read it aloud first and then encourage the child to help you read it next time. If the sentences are very simple and consist mainly of familiar words you may find that, after talking about the pictures, the child wants to read it for himself without your help. Some children will respond enthusiastically to a challenge like 'would you like to have a go at reading this line to me?' Others might feel alarmed that you appear to expect so much of them. Many may need to be eased in more gently. You might casually point to a word asking 'Can you tell me what that says?' and take it from there.

How to lead your child is very much a matter for your own intuition based on your special knowledge and relationship. But as long as the child is enthusiastic and confident and your approach is positive and encouraging, things are obviously going all right.

When he is on the brink of making this breakthrough, a child could attempt to read something that is far too difficult for him. You may have to ease his frustration and move him on to something easier. It is worth having a few spare easy readers tucked away for just such a situation.

Once your child has managed his first reader he may feel quite pleased with himself and want to read it to you— and everyone else—very often. That's fine but do not let him get stuck on this achievement. Find another book that really interests him and encourage him to move on.

Practising

Keep the games going for as long as the child enjoys them and adapt them to give him a chance to practise the new words he is meeting in his books. How often he reads to you is a matter for individual choice but a few minutes a day (longer if the child wants) split into a couple of sessions is probably enough for most children. Continue reading the bedtime story.

When the child reads to you ensure that the atmosphere is relaxed and loving with as few distractions as possible. The child should be physically comfortable and feel happy and secure. As with the games, always end when on a high note—don't be tempted to go on too long.

Mistakes

A secure child can take risks and does not worry about making mistakes. Mistakes in fact often provide a useful insight into how the child's mind is working. If he makes many mistakes then you should give him a simpler book or he may become discouraged.

When he reads a word wrongly try and see *why* as this will help you to help him.

There are several causes for mis-reading a word:

● He may confuse it with a similar word.
● He may notice the first letter (or the last letter or a letter combination inside the word) and make a hasty guess.
● Perhaps he has 'read' the picture and anticipated the story.
● His mind might be jumping ahead of his reading and he is making up his own story.

When you spot a logical reason for a mistake be positive and give credit for it:

'That's good you've noticed that word is like . . . but it can't be . . .

because . . .' or 'That's a good guess because the word here begins with **m** and the word you've said begins with **m** but let's look at it more carefully.'

Meeting new words

As the child reads more books he is going to come across more words which you have not already taught him. Knowing whether and how to help is a matter in which your own sensitivity will best guide you, and you should judge the situation according to the child's mood, the word, and how absorbed he is in the story.

When he comes across a word which brings him to a standstill you might react in any of the following ways:

● Tell him the word straightaway (if he is very absorbed in the story or is unlikely to work it out for himself).
● Wait and see if he can work it out himself. It is important to give him time to think without any pressure.
● Offer some help—go over the letters with him—look at the picture—point out where the word has appeared before.

Make a mental note of any words that need going over and when you come to the end of a page do a bit of quick

In some situations a child will guess correctly at the meaning of words he cannot read.

revision. Point to words at random and ask the child to read them, include plenty of easy ones so that he does not become discouraged.

Let him have a turn at pointing out words for you to read. Give him a silly answer occasionally to make him laugh and keep him on his toes. You might also try just saying a word and seeing if he can find it on the page.

After a time you might find that the child can dispense with pointing at every word as he reads. A piece of card held under the line of print will help to stop

his eye straying. The card can also serve as a book mark and you might write on it any new words.

When he does not recognise a word encourage your child to scan to the end of the sentence to help him guess it.

As your child reads more you are continually going to encounter the problem of speaking a language with a very erratic spelling. Consider for instance how there are seven different ways of making the **oo** sound in the following words:

to too two shoe stew blue through

Knowing individual letters is only going to give minimal help with these words, and many other eccentric spellings, such as:

though night could where

The child really has to learn these as sight words, as he did the Look and Say words.

Each time he encounters a new word with difficult spelling, help him to fix it in his mind by using it in Look and Say games or Reading in Action ideas as often as you can. If you can reinforce his learning by repeating his experience of this word he should soon get it clear.

Reading with Expression

When he is learning a child may concentrate so hard on the individual words that his reading is jerky or expressionless. Help him to get over this. Look at these four areas to see where you can give help most effectively.

● **Imitation**—If you read aloud from his book and ask him to read it after you, this will help him to feel the flow of the words. Remember that you are your child's reading model so be sure that your own reading is expressive. Try not to feel self-conscious.

● **Understanding**—Does your child understand what he is reading? If the words are beyond comfortable range then reading fluency will be affected.

● **Relaxation**—Is the child happy and physically comfortable? Check that he is sitting comfortably. Is his breathing smooth? Children sometimes expect to get too much mileage out of a single breath.

● **Scanning**—Pointing at individual words may slow down the eye. Try out the piece of card as suggested on the previous page and encourage him to scan a sentence silently before reading it aloud.

Reading with expression prevents the listeners from becoming bored and can really fire a child's imagination and enthusiasm for a story.

Magic 'e'

This is the **e** at the end of words like **gate, line, ride** where the **e** remains silent itself but makes the previous vowel sound long. When your child learned the letter sounds he learned the short sounds of the vowels—**a** as in **hat**, **e** as in **bed**, **i** as in **fit**, **o** as in **log**, **u** as in **bus**. Since then he has probably encountered words where the vowels have their long sounds, as in **baby, read, hide, go, blue**. You may have had to help him out with words such as these and tell him that sometimes **a** says its name **ay** or that **e** says its name **ee**.

When magic 'e' words begin to appear in his reading then it is time to introduce him to this exciting letter!

You should only tackle magic 'e' with an older child or one who has quite a lot of reading experience. As it is always advisable to link new material to familiar information, refer to your note book or box of word cards and see what magic 'e' words have already been encountered and use these as examples.

The list below gives pairs of words before and after the magic 'e' treatment. Your child may not be familiar with some of the words so you will need to select from it when you play the game.

cap cape   can cane   fin fine
hop hope   fir fire   tub tube
tim time   hat hate
pip pipe   pin pine   bit bite

To introduce him to the idea of magic 'e' lay out the letter cards for one of the three-letter words above. Let him read it to you and then add on a letter **e** at the end and read the new word to him. Do this with several of the words. You can explain to him how magic 'e' makes the **i** in **pipe** say its name or the **a** in **cape** says its name. But avoid any over elaborate explanation.

MAGIC 'e' ARE YOU WITHIN?

You will need
  Word cards for some of the three-letter words in the list above
    Letter **e** card for each word
    Blank letter cards
    Bag

Method
1. Share out the word cards between the players and put the **e** cards and blanks into a bag.
2. The first player dips into the bag saying, 'Magic 'e' are you within?'
3. He draws out a card. If he has an **e** he places it on the end of one of his three-letter words saying 'Magic 'e', magic 'e', change my **pip** to **pipe** for me.' Or something to that effect!

When a player draws a blank he cannot go that turn. The winner is the one who first gets a magic 'e' on all his words.

Writing

In general the manual skill required for the writing of words develops more slowly than the ability to read them. So do not expect that your child will be able to write at the same level (if at all) as he can read. Should he show an interest in writing you might find the following suggestions helpful. Most pre-school children will probably enjoy the pattern exercises which will help their manual control.

Pattern making

The formation of letters is based on combinations of certain recurring patterns mainly:

circles (or parts of them)

vertical lines

hooks

arches

zigzags

In fact, any regular patterns help a child to increase his control. Try some of the ideas and make up your own.

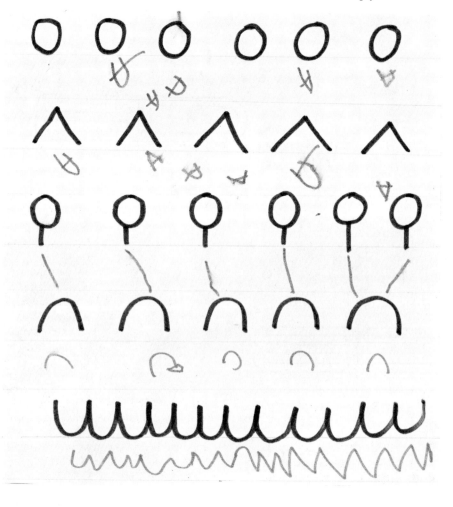

92

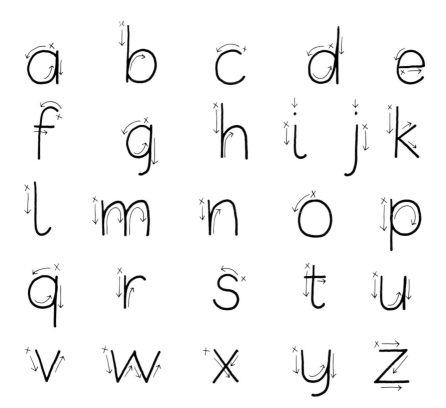

Letters

If you are going to teach letters do check with the diagram that you are forming them accurately yourself. Most of us pick up a few bad writing habits over a lifetime and it would be unfortunate to pass them on to our children.

In teaching writing emphasis must always be placed on the correct way to form the letters. Although a child may arrive at a letter that looks acceptable, unless he learns how to form it properly he will have difficulties later especially when he starts to learn joined-up writing.

You could start off by using a sand or salt tray. Sprinkle some dry sand or salt to cover the bottom of a baking tray and draw a letter in it with your finger.

As he gains in control a child may enjoy tracing letters or his name. Write the letter or name boldly in felt pen and secure greaseproof paper over it with paper clips.

A variation on tracing is to write lightly in pencil and let the child go over it with crayon or felt pen.

You can also indicate a letter with dots or dashes which the child joins together.

Once the child has mastered the writing of several letters try this exercise which combines writing with phonic work: onto a large sheet of paper draw some object or glue some cut-outs. Write the word beside each but put a dash in place of the first letter. The child writes in the first letter.

Other Reading Methods

Here is a brief outline of three reading methods that have not been used in this book. It is not suggested that you should try them. They are only included for your interest.

Alphabetic Method

This method emphasises the *names* of letters and not their *sounds*. (The Phonic approach uses the sounds of letters.) In the Alphabetic method letters are pronounced as **ay bee see dee ee** (**a b c d e**).

You only have to sound out a simple word like **cat** 'see-ay-tee' to realise how unhelpful this method is.

Use of colour

Several schemes have been devised which use coloured letters to indicate the particular sound of that letter in a word.

Initial Teaching Alphabet i.t.a.

The Initial Teaching Alphabet or i.t.a. is a reading aid rather than a reading method as it still has to be taught using the Look and Say or Phonic approach.

It was designed to simplify the complexities of English spelling and has 45 characters in all. It has no capital letters. In traditional lettering one letter may have several possible sounds depending on the word it is in; in i.t.a. a different symbol is given for each different sound.

In the event of i.t.a. being used at your child's future school (and you will almost certainly hear about it if it is) it is probably better not to tackle these games.

Children using i.t.a. can only read from specially printed material until they transfer to the traditional alphabet. This is one of the reasons why it is not widely used.

The characters of the initial teaching alphabet.

a apple	ɑ father	æ angel	au author	b bed	c cat	ꜿh chair
d doll	ɛɛ eel	e egg	f finger	g girl	h hat	ie tie
i ink	j jam	k kitten	l lion	m man	n nest	ŋ king
œ toe	o on	ꙍ book	ꙍ food	ou out	oi oil	p pig
r red	ɾ bird	s soap	ʃh ship	ʒ treasure	t tree	th three
th mother	ue due	u up	v van	w window	wh wheel	y yellow
z zoo	ʃ is					

Books to read

Here are some simple picture books published by Simon & Schuster Young Books for you to enjoy reading:–

Caspar's Week
Written by Cindy Ward · Illustrated by Tomie de Poala
Young children will love following Caspar's escapades and learning the days of the week at the same time.
Hardback ISBN 0 356 16783 6   **Paperback** 0 356 16784 4

Where are my Bananas?
Written by M. Christina Butler · Illustrated by Meg Rutherford
Elephant, Bear, Tiger, Monkey and Mouse pack a basket with food and set off for a picnic.
A delightful story and memory game.
Hardback ISBN 0 356 16813 1   **Paperback** ISBN 0 356 16814 X

The Boy
Written and illustrated by Paul Dowling
The boy is being pursued and narrowly escapes capture by the wild menagerie of monsters running after him. His clothes are not so lucky and fall victim to the happily snapping jaws of his pursuers. But is the warm fur coat he finds as harmless as it looks?
Hardback ISBN 0 671 69703 X

The Cat Sat on the Rat
Written by George Adams · Illustrated by Annie Axworthy
Cat's efforts to retrieve his hat which has blown away are helped none too successfully by a variety of animal friends. A zany tale with a picture word list to aid vocabulary building.
Paperback 0 356 16037 8

Melvin's Cold Feet
Written by Linda Crust · Illustrated by John Brindle
Melvin mouse was born with very cold feet which are a problem. Luckily when it comes to finding somewhere warm to live, he meets a friendly spider who helps him out.
Hardback ISBN 0 7500 0196 8   **Paperback** ISBN 0 356 16746 1

Hello Mr Scarecrow
This simple but vivid story describes a year in the life of cheerful Mr Scarecrow.
Hardback ISBN 0356 11798 7   **Paperback** ISBN 0 7500 0194 1

Friska the Sheep that was too Small
Friska, the smallest sheep in the flock, is teased by all the other sheep. One day a hungry wolf finds the flock and Friska has a chance to prove that bigger isn't always better.
Hardback ISBN 0 356 13049 5   **Paperback** ISBN 0 356 13050 9

I Wish I Liked Rice Pudding
Written by Joyce Dunbar · Illustrated by Carol Thompson
An amusing story of a spirited little girl's likes and dislikes, sunny moods and tantrums!
Hardback ISBN 0 671 69948 2

Published by Simon & Schuster Young Books and available from all good bookshops.

Index of Games

Acknowledgements

The author and publishers wish to thank the following people and organisations for the help they have given in the preparation of this book and for allowing their material to be reproduced:

Betty Root, Centre for the Teaching of Reading, University of Reading.

Michelle Ehrenmark, Crouch Hall Road Day Nursery, London N8

All the friends who have given advice and help with this book and to those who have allowed themselves to be photographed.

page 13 (top) Frederick Warne (Publishers) Ltd. for permission to reproduce pages 6 and 7 of *Words and Pictures People* by Margaret Clarke.

page 13 (bottom) Hart-Davis Educational for permission to reproduce page 4 of One Two Three and Away Introductory Book *J Roger and the Little Mouse* by Sheila McCullagh.

page 14 Macmillan Educational for permission to reproduce page 1 of *King Dan, the Dane* by Terry Reid from the Language in Action series.

page 15 Ginn & Co. Ltd. for permission to reproduce page 11 of *I can read* by Theodore Clymer, Level 3, Book 3 in the Ginn Reading Programme-Reading 360.

page 18 Schoolmaster Publishing Co. Ltd. for permission to reproduce the Key Words Chart from *Key Words to Literacy* by J. McNally and W. Murray.

pages 85 & 90 (photographs) Joan Dashwood, The Rainbow Bookshop, Walton-on-Thames, Surrey.

page 86 (photograph) Heffer's Children's Bookshop, Cambridge.